ANYPLACE BUT HERE

ANYPLACE BUT HERE

Young, Alone, and Homeless: What to Do

Ellen Switzer

Atheneum · 1992 · New York

Maxwell Macmillan Canada
Toronto
Maxwell Macmillan International
New York   Oxford   Singapore   Sydney

Atheneum
Macmillan Publishing Company
866 Third Avenue
New York, NY 10022

Maxwell Macmillan Canada, Inc.
1200 Eglinton Avenue East
Suite 200
Don Mills, Ontario M3C 3N1

Macmillan Publishing Company is part of the Maxwell Communication Group of Companies.

First edition

Printed in the United States of America
10 9 8 7 6 5 4 3 2 1
The text of this book is set in 12/15 Times Roman.

Library of Congress Cataloging-in-Publication Data

Switzer, Ellen Eichenwald.
   Anyplace but here: young, alone, and homeless: what to do
Ellen Switzer.
      p.   cm.
   Summary: Examines the problems that lead young people to live on the streets and what life is like for them there. Also provides information on how they can get help.
   ISBN 0–689–31694–1
   1. Runaway teenagers—United States—Juvenile literature. 2. Runaway children—United States—Juvenile literature. [1. Runaways. 2. Family problems.] I. Title.
HV1431.S95   1992
   362.7′4—dc20   92–15

TABLE OF CONTENTS

v

CONTENTS

INTRODUCTION

When I first started to do research for this book, I was sure that the fact gathering would be fairly simple. I had seen children and teenagers living in the streets of New York for several years, and realized that their numbers were increasing. Friends had told me that many young people were living, alone or in groups, in other large urban centers throughout the United States.

I thought that I would go to agencies working with troubled young people, talk to social workers, teachers, psychologists, and others who might know the extent of the problem—the reasons why so many kids were leaving their homes—and get suggestions as to what individual children and adults might do to work out their difficulties at home, rather than in a homeless shelter or on a city street. I also thought that I could meet with youngsters in shelters and group homes who would tell me their own stories.

Most of these assumptions turned out to be wrong. The research for this book turned out to be much more difficult than I had imagined. In the first place, there are few sources of help, either public or private, for homeless children. In the second place, many of the young people living alone in the streets of our cities have, understandably, become suspicious and angry. They suspect almost every adult who asks too many questions, since many adults have exploited them, blamed them for situations that were not their fault, and, almost always, tried to get them to go somewhere else. It's known as the "not in my back-yard," or "NIMBY," attitude. Homeless kids, just like homeless adults, are not welcome in most of our cities and towns. For many of those whose job it is to help, the first priority is to find a way to get children with no home passed along to some other authority, preferably out of town or out of state. Most urban communities in this country are very short of funds, and helping a homeless minor often turns out to be even more expensive than helping a homeless adult or family.

So homeless young people will hesitate before talking to adults. Even if they talk, they are careful to limit their stories in ways that makes it difficult to identify their parents, guardians, and even their hometowns. Most who live on the streets for more than a few days have reasons for not wanting to go back home: They were sexually, physically, or mentally abused, and life at home seems even more impossible than it does on a street in New York, Los Angeles, San Francisco, Boston, or some other big city. Indeed, most of these street children have picked a big city because they don't want to be found.

Even those who have managed to get to a safe haven in a group home or a large dormitory facility don't want to talk. Many feel that if they tell the truth about themselves and the ways they have been forced to cope, they will be sent away. So when one meets runaways in a group along with a representative of the organization that is sheltering them, they tend to echo whatever the "official" adult chooses to tell a reporter about the purposes, success, and organization of their present home away from home.

Finally I decided that the only way to talk to these young people was to meet them on their own, on the streets, in coffee shops and other hangouts they frequent, or in the shelters they themselves had found in abandoned houses, in railroad and bus stations, and in other places where they felt that they were not under the supervision of someone who might use information they gave about themselves against them.

During the two years I worked on this book, I spent many evenings and nights on the streets in New York and other cities finding street children who would talk to me after I had established that I would not report anything they told me to any authority or to their families, unless I had their permission to do so. I told everybody I interviewed the truth: I was a reporter writing a book. I also assured them that I would change names, hometowns or other identifying facts if they asked me to do so. Most did. There were a few who talked to me because they wanted help to go home or to get referrals to sources of help for specific problems such as illness, pregnancy, or one of the most frequently cited reasons—fear of "going crazy." When I was asked for help, I did what I could to see to it that the person who requested it got to the best possible source of help: hospital emergency rooms, food banks, counseling, child welfare departments, shelters, etc.

For those who clearly did not want to make contact with any agency or professional, I tried to provide food, clothing, and sometimes money to help during a temporary crisis. Reporters are not in the advice-giving business. When dealing with adults, they are supposed to keep personal feelings and opinions out of their relationships with those about whom they write. With children, this was often impossible. I have children and grandchildren of my own, and to keep all relationships completely impersonal sometimes seemed just plain wrong. I did, however, keep all promises of confidentiality, even though this meant that I could not check the information the children gave me about themselves. I have used only those stories and that information that I believe to be true after repeatedly talking to a child or teenager.

During my years of research on this book, I followed about twenty-five street children in New York. I met with them, first two or three times a week, and then once a month, whenever possible. I got to know them very well, and they got to know me. I still check with them to make sure that they are not sick, in trouble with the police, or so depressed that they can no longer cope.

It was often frustrating and saddening not to be able to do more, even for those who I felt had become my friends. But I now know, from experience, that any individual, working alone, can do very little to change these tragic lives.

What I can do is write this book so that if you, or perhaps someone you know, is considering leaving home because "anyplace but here" seems an improvement, you will think twice before buying that bus ticket to an unknown future without money, without a place to stay, without a job, and without friends. Getting help in one's hometown is almost always easier than in a strange city. In this book you will find sources of help for general and specific family and personal problems. Trying to change the situation at home with the assistance of a professional should always be the first, not the last, resort for anyone who is truly unhappy at home. And help will often be available more easily if one is still at home than if one has become just one of a huge army of homeless kids on the streets.

PART ONE

THE RUNAWAYS—
WHO THEY ARE
AND HOW THEY LIVE

CHAPTER 1

MY OWN STORY

When I was fifteen years old, I ran away from home. It was certainly not a spur-of-the-moment decision. I had been saving every penny that I had earned baby-sitting, leaf raking, and doing other chores around my quiet suburban neighborhood, and putting them in what I referred to in my mind as "the getaway fund." The money was hidden under an old pair of socks in my underwear drawer and had been accumulating for over three years. Even today, looking back after half a century, my decision does not seem irrational. It was, however, unrealistic and self-defeating, a fact I realized within hours, before anyone in my family had even discovered I had gone.

The reason for my desperate desire to get away from home is irrelevant now. Both my parents are dead, and I have come to understand why they often acted the way they did. But taking off into an unknown, dangerous future was no solution, as the one person whom I called from the bus station (just before I bought a ticket to Boston, my eventual destination) pointed out to me in no uncertain terms.

She explained to me that even if I felt there was no place worse than my seemingly normal but deeply unhappy home, what was waiting for me on the other end of the bus ride would almost certainly be worse. What's more, running away was no way to prepare me for a different kind of life.

The person I called was a woman I admired very much, a role model for me and many of the other girls who lived in our neighborhood. She was a lawyer who worked with families and children in trouble, the mother of one of my friends, and someone who was always ready to listen to the problems of her own three children and those of the rest of us who dropped in when we needed someone to help us sort out our difficulties. She treated us as people, not children, and actually rarely gave advice. She did, however, often present us with alternatives to our problems. She presented us not with ready-made answers, but with new ways of thinking.

This time she *did* give advice, firmly and rationally. "In most states, running away from home is considered an act of juvenile delinquency," she told me. "If you are found on a city street, with no place to go and very little money, you will almost certainly be picked up by the police and either sent back to your parents or to some kind of juvenile detention center. I know that things at home are very difficult for you, but until you have graduated from high school, you are best off at home. After graduation, I will help you to get away legally . . . either to a college or to a job. You can be declared 'an emancipated minor' at that point and be free to go wherever you want, as long as you are self-supporting. A college scholarship would do that for you. If you need a lawyer, you can count on my help—free of charge."

I shall be forever grateful to that woman. She kept me from wrecking my future (juvenile convictions don't get you scholarships) and kept all her other promises too. When I had graduated from high school, she spoke to my father and told him that unless he allowed me to leave voluntarily, she would get me a court hearing. Then she helped me get a full scholarship at the college from which she had graduated by talking to the admissions and scholarship committee heads and explaining my situation. Several years later she would receive an honorary degree from that college while I sat in the audience applauding as loudly as I could.

My second experience occurred when I was married, with two sons of my own. In my way I had tried to emulate the woman who had helped me. I listened to the problems of children from unhappy homes who now came to me for advice. Most just needed a few days away from a tense family situation, and we had an extra bedroom. I would call the parents and invite the youngster to stay with us for a week until things at home had cooled down enough for everybody to act in a more constructive way. In many cases, I advised counseling, not just for the "bad" child, but for the whole family. I worked for a counseling agency as a volunteer, and it was amazing what a few sessions with an experienced and trained professional could do to help relieve even serious tensions.

One day a fifteen-year-old boy who was in my younger son's high school class rang our doorbell. I will call him Don, although like all the names of troubled children in this book, that's not what he was really called. He had run away from home six months earlier and now was staying with several other boys and girls about his age in an abandoned beach-front cottage in the small Connecticut town where we lived. His family apparently had made little effort to try to find him. He was known as the community troublemaker, had been suspended from school several times, and there were rumors that he had once produced a marijuana cigarette on the school bus.

Now he was in real trouble. Several summer houses that had been boarded up for the winter had been broken into and burglarized during the past few months. Most contained few if any valuables, but one

6

house belonged to an antiques collector, who was careless enough to leave some of his best pieces in an empty house over the winter.

Don had been seen in the neighborhood with several of the other teenagers from his hideaway, and the police found one missing chair in his home away from home. He was arrested, his parents were called, and he had just finished his first juvenile court hearing that day. As it turned out, all the other missing antiques were found in an abandoned lot. Don and his friends swore that they had found the chair there and had taken it home because, apparently, nobody wanted it. The judge was skeptical, but there was not enough proof to convict anybody. He did, however, tell Don that he would either have to go home to his parents or find a "respectable, supervised" place to live. "Would you be considered respectable by a court?" he asked me. That, obviously, was a plea for him to be allowed to stay with us. I asked him why he didn't want to go home instead. He took off his shirt and showed me the reasons: whip marks and scars all over his back. His father was a child abuser who took out his drunken rages on Don.

My husband and I talked the situation over with our younger son, who had rather admired Don's independent spirit for some time, and we agreed that he could live with us if he promised not to get into any more trouble and to return to school. Drugs were out. Alcohol was out. Running away was out. For the time being a weekday curfew of ten o'clock was in. Homework was definitely in. Don was a very bright boy with a talent for drawing and writing. He had every chance of graduating with good enough grades to get a college scholarship. His personality problems were obviously caused, at least in part, by his impossible father.

I told Don that I would have to report the abuse to the agency where I worked and that one of the staff members would talk to him and his father. The staff member became convinced that the father had indeed beaten Don for years. He had also abused his wife, who was too terrified of him to leave or to call the authorities. The counselor pointed out to the father that under Connecticut law there was an obligation to report the abuse to the child welfare authorities. This he did. Within a year Don's mother had left her husband, taking her daughter with her but leaving Don with us.

He stayed in our house until he graduated from high school and got himself a scholarship at a state college. There were times when my husband and I wished that we had never agreed to the situation in the first place, but on the whole there were fewer problems than we had expected. Don regularly raided the refrigerator, sometimes just before a dinner party. In minutes he could turn a reasonably orderly room into something that looked as if it had been hit by a band of burglars plus a hurricane. He left paint

8

spots all over our furniture . . . but then, both of my sons had been guilty of similar annoyances.

The last time I saw Don was the evening after my husband had suddenly died. He arrived with a truck full of wood for our fireplace, which he carefully stacked at our front door. "I can't see you chopping wood, Ellen," he said. "And you have no idea how expensive that stuff is." Then he went over my house, carefully trying out window and door locks. "You know, you must have the least burglarproof house in Connecticut," he informed me. When I asked how he could tell, he said, "Never mind; let's just try to fix it." He came back, installed new locks on the doors and inside fasteners on all the downstairs windows. He also brought a smoke alarm and carefully installed it over the staircase. Then he made himself a cup of tea and split. I have never seen him since, although my son occasionally meets him in New York, where Don is now in the antiques business and doing rather well.

My other direct experience with a runaway happened a few years ago. I now spend a good deal of time in New York City, staying in a small studio apartment near the United Nations. During one especially cold winter I noticed a boy, who looked to be about nine years old, standing at various street corners on Second Avenue, where there are many expensive and elegant restaurants and bars. The boy would approach cars, usually with only the driver inside, and exchange a few words. Sometimes he would get into the car and drive off. A few hours later he was usually back at the street corner, looking for more customers. AIDS had already become one of the most frequent killers of children and teenagers, and this boy was putting himself in danger every evening of his life. It was obvious that he was living in the streets and selling himself.

One day when it was snowing and there were few cars driving by, I approached him and asked if he'd like to go to a local coffee shop for a hamburger and some hot chocolate. Obviously, he was in a situation of extreme danger and nobody had tried to do anything about it. He looked me over suspiciously, but since I was clearly not the type to belong either to the police or the welfare department, and getting out of the cold did seem like a good idea, he came with me.

He told me that his street name was "Beau" ("That means 'pretty' in French. Somebody told me that."). He was indeed attractive, and he assured me "almost twelve years old." He had been on the streets for a year.

He wore expensive jeans, a leather jacket, and several chains that looked like real gold around his neck. I told him that I had observed what he was doing, and I pointed out the dangers to him. He certainly knew about AIDS but insisted that nobody as young and healthy as he could ever get it. I had

10

brought along a whole envelope full of material to try to persuade him otherwise. He flat-out refused to believe me. "I know hundreds of kids who work the way I do, and none of them has AIDS," he said. "Besides, by the time I can get it, there will probably be a cure."

I tried to persuade him that he was also in other kinds of constant danger. Even if by some stroke of luck he didn't catch the deadly human immunodeficiency virus, HIV, which can cause AIDS, there were men who were sadists and who might hurt or even kill him. Beau said that he knew a lot about the people he picked up and that he was careful not to "get mixed up with a nut." When I tried to continue the conversation, he stopped me. "Lady, how much money do you make a week?" he asked me. I told him. "I make at least three times that much . . . in a bad week," he said. "I think I have a better job than you do. I'm smart. Do you see any other kids like me in this neighborhood? They're all hanging around Times Square where the money is not nearly as good, and it really can be dangerous . . . especially if you wear gold chains and carry cash around." He pulled out a roll of ten-dollar bills, insisted on paying for both our meals, and disappeared into the snowy night. I saw him a few more times and we waved at each other.

There was nothing I could do about him except to call the police, who would have put him in New

York City's juvenile hall for a few days, and then probably would just have let him go. His family in North Carolina didn't want him around, he had told me. "They think I'm a fag and a worthless bum." Before talking to him, I had already called several welfare agencies who indicated that perhaps sometime in the future, when their waiting list was down or when someone had the time to come over to the East Side of New York, they might look into the situation.

Eventually he disappeared. He may have found a location where there were more and richer customers. He may have gotten sick. He may even be dead. Nobody who had the power to do something about Beau had apparently done anything constructive. I checked with the police and with child welfare to find out if they knew what had happened to him. Nobody did.

Then I remembered the "hundreds of kids" he had told me hung out around Times Square. I am a reporter, and it seemed like an interesting story to find out how and whether these children survived, who they were, where they came from, and why they were living under such terrible conditions. I went to Times Square one night and saw the homeless children—at every street corner, in front of every porno theater, huddled on heating grates in the sidewalk—and started talking to them. Eventually I came to know some of them. That's when I started to write this book. Someone needed to tell their story. And more than that, someone needed to let potential runaways know what life was really like on the streets and give them some viable alternatives.

CHAPTER 2

WHO ARE THEY?

In 1990 in the United States, about one million children between the ages of eight and seventeen were living in the streets. Some runaways return home on their own after a week or two. Others are found and returned to their hometowns and their families against their will. Still others are not found for months or years. And too many are found, but their families do not want them back. In many cases they have not actually run away from home at all: They have been pushed out with little or no money and no idea of where they are going.

Together, these make up the children and adolescents who live in the streets or abandoned places of our cities, with no home, no adult help or guidance, no medical care, no sex education, no one to turn to, even in times of serious illness or other trouble. The adults they meet, often drug dealers or pimps, exploit them. They have learned to distrust almost everybody, and usually with good reason.

When they left their usually deeply disturbed homes, their one thought was that life had to be better "almost anywhere but here." But living in the streets, they come to know that life can actually get worse, and most of them begin desperately searching for help in finding some other place for themselves because they have learned through bitter experience that survival in the streets is marginal, at best. Then when they say "anyplace but here," they mean they'd like to get away from that grate on which they are sleeping because a little warmth seeps through on a freezing cold night, that doorway in which they are standing to get a cooler breeze from the air-conditioning inside on broiling hot days, the garbage pails from which they often scavenge for food. They have come to realize that the only way they can survive at all is to sell one of the two commodities for which there always seems to be a market: drugs or their own bodies.

All kinds of kids run away. There is no special "type." They come from all kinds of backgrounds, all races (although in some parts of the country a surprisingly large number are from so-called middle-class homes), and all areas of the United States: cities, small towns, farms, and rural villages. They run for a vast number of causes. Few who stay in the streets

15

for longer than one or two weeks don't have under-standable reasons for their flight.

Here are a few of the children I met when I first went out into the streets myself to talk to those who left home in hopes of a better life "anyplace but here":

Egypt

She called herself "Egypt" after her favorite char-acter in a daytime soap. She told everyone who asked that she was eighteen years old. After three ham-burgers and four cups of hot chocolate in an off-Times Square coffee shop, she reluctantly gave her real first name: Margaret (or "Maggie, as Mom used to call me before they took her away to the hospital"). A few talks later she confided her real age: fourteen on her last birthday.

Dressed in the uniform of New York's street pros-titutes—a minimal fake leather skirt, a ratty-looking fur jacket (also fake), and a see-through blouse—she spent most of her time standing near a porno theater waiting for customers. They usually passed her by because even with high heels, a badly-fitting dark wig, which covered her straight blond hair, and layers of makeup, she looked like the lost child she was. The men who picked her up seemed to realize that this youngster didn't know her way around the sex scene yet. They also tended to treat her very badly. She said she liked older men . . . they reminded her of the time she had a father. When she talked about where she came from and how she got where she was, she started to weep. Her mascara ran down her face, making black lines.

Maggie lived for the first ten years of her life on a family farm in Idaho with her parents and her two younger brothers. She loved the farm and her family. There was no other life she wanted. She was planning to finish high school and eventually marry a farmer, raise cattle and wheat, plant a large vegetable garden, and have at least three children, just as her mother and grandmother had.

But during the farm depression of the last decade, her parents went bankrupt, and their land, home, and all their possessions were sold at auction.

Her father, feeling unbearably depressed and guilty at having lost everything that had been handed down to him from his parents and grandparents, committed suicide. Her mother had a complete emotional breakdown and was committed to a state hospital for the mentally ill.

Maggie tried to keep what was left of her family together. She and her two brothers hid in a neighbor's hayloft and picked up scraps of food wherever they could. After two weeks, they were found by "someone who said she was a social worker," and placed in separate foster homes. Maggie tried to stay in touch with her brothers, but they were moved over and over again, until she could no longer find them. Her mother did not answer her letters. When she called the hospital, she was told that she could not visit.

The foster home in which Maggie was placed had apparently not been investigated very carefully by any of the understaffed, overworked agencies that were suddenly responsible for hundreds of children from bankrupt farm families.

In Maggie's town, there was only one part-time, untrained woman finding places for homeless children. So the couple with whom Maggie lived used her as an unpaid maid and farmhand. She was allowed no time to herself. Often she was even prevented from going to school because she had not finished her chores. And, although she had once loved school and had done well, she didn't care about education any longer. Her clothes were secondhand and badly kept. She was often too exhausted to follow what the teacher was saying. Once she went to sleep in the middle of a class and was accused of using drugs . . . although she was simply tired because she had been asked to do all the cleaning and cooking in the house during the harvest season.

She tried to complain to the woman who had placed her in that "home." But she was told not to complain. She was told she ought to be grateful to the "fine people who charitably had taken her in." So she stayed until the seventeen-year-old son of a neighbor raped her. Her foster parents insisted that she had "seduced" him, and that on top of being lazy and worthless, she was also a whore. They also told her that if she did not stop bothering them and the boy's parents, they would see to it that she was sent to an institution for juvenile delinquents. That is when she took a few ten-dollar bills that she found hidden in a cookbook, got on a bus, and went to New York.

When I spoke to her, she had been in the city for a year. At first she tried to get a job . . . any job. She looked at HELP WANTED signs in the windows of fast-food shops and supermarkets. But she was too young to get a work permit. She could not go to school because she had no address, and she was terrified that, if she asked for help from any agency or the police, she would be sent back to Idaho, where, as promised by her foster family, she would be sent to a reformatory. After all, they now could add theft to all the other charges they might file against her.

Although she could not get any kind of real job or find a way to get an education, a pimp did not consider her too young to work. But she had heard about pimps from some of the other girls on the streets . . . they give their charges a place to sleep and money for food but expected them to bring in a big profit from prostitution; if they didn't, they might be beaten. A story had made the rounds among some of the youngsters at Maggie's street corner that one

19

pimp had actually killed several girls who had proved to be unsatisfactory money-makers. So far Maggie had avoided pimps. She changed her location when she was approached by a would-be pimp—or just ran away.

Maggie had been approached several times with offers to sell drugs. She knew that she could make more money that way, but she also knew how dangerous dealing could be. She was even more afraid of drug dealers than she was of policemen who might send her back to Idaho. "People get shot all the time around here, and it usually has something to do with drugs," she said.

What was to become of Maggie? Unless she got some kind of help, she would probably start taking drugs eventually, just to make her existence bearable. She might also become seriously ill.

"Maggie, unless she gets off the streets, won't survive another year," one of the older, more sophisticated girls who also worked her corner said. "She's still too straight to make it in this kind of life." Maggie was still too much the farm girl her early life had prepared her to be.

In time, there was an improvement in her situation. She found a group of youngsters who had created, in an abandoned building, a kind of informal group home for themselves. The kids, who ranged in age from fourteen to seventeen, lived together, pooled their money, and took care of each other as best they could. The last time I saw Maggie before writing this book, that's where she was. Eventually, that building will be torn down as part of the new Times Square improvement project. Also, the city had begun searching abandoned buildings regularly, emptying them of their occupants, because the authorities rightly believed that life there is dangerous. There have been many fires. Kids cook on old grates, because there are no stoves. They light oil lamps and heaters because there is no heat and electricity. But they are still better off than they were before they found their home away from home, and, when the city officials say that they are going to move the kids out, one might well ask, "Out where?" Certainly Maggie will not choose to go back to Idaho.

Al

Al is short for Alfredo, the name of his father, and he was sixteen years old. When I came to know him, he was living with a group of other adolescents under the Sunset Boulevard overpass in Los Angeles. Four years before he had lived in Boston, in his grandmother's tenement apartment. His father came from an ethnic Italian family, his mother from an African-American one. His parents had a brief and secret love affair in junior high school. His mother was thirteen, his father fifteen. When she got pregnant, Alfredo senior disappeared. "Your mother told me he didn't really want to leave her, but the family just moved away," Al's grandmother told him. "They certainly didn't want to take on the problem of my daughter's baby." Neither, it turned out, did anybody else. Al's grandmother told him that the one agency to which her pregnant teenage daughter went for counseling assured her that terminating the pregnancy would be a serious mistake. "There are thousands of wonderful couples looking for children to adopt," she was told. "Many spend years trying to find a baby. Your child will have a good home with parents who love him."

What nobody bothered to explain was that, although there are indeed thousands of couples looking for adoptable babies, they mean white, healthy newborns. There are almost no homes for an interracial child, especially one with a mother who gives birth prematurely at fourteen, because would-be adoptive parents fear birth defects. Al was born in the seventh month of his mother's pregnancy and spent almost a year in the hospital before he was considered well enough to leave. And there were no eager adoptive parents waiting for him, so the hospital gave him back to his mom.

She moved him into the already overcrowded apartment with her mother, her three sisters and one brother, and, as his grandmother told Al, "tried to take care of him and love him." But for a fifteen-year-old, the burdens of being a mother were too much. One day she disappeared, probably joining the army of street children to which her son now belonged. Nobody had heard from her since, although her mother reported her as missing to the police and tried herself to find her by calling all her friends and looking in all the teenage hangouts she knew her daughter liked.

So Al grew up in his grandmother's home, not too unhappily at first. She was a kind, loving woman, he says, who would not have abandoned him even if he made her already difficult life more complicated. But he knew he wasn't really wanted. Sometimes when his grandmother thought he couldn't hear her, she referred to him as "my daughter's mistake." But he made a few friends, went to a neighborhood school, and did well in most of his subjects. He loved music and taught himself to play the guitar that his absent mother had once owned. Also, he made up songs, which he sang to himself whenever he got sad.

Everything changed when he had to transfer to junior high. The neighborhood in which he grew up was largely black, but it was right next to an area that was mostly Italian. Probably his father had grown up there. At any rate, the area was overrun by two gangs: one black and one Italian, who periodically attacked each other or each other's members. Al began to find out how difficult his interracial background really was. Neither gang wanted him. Each thought he belonged to the other, and he was periodically beaten by members of both.

When he started high school, the gang violence became much worse. Now the members carried guns rather than just baseball bats, knives, and brass knuckles. There were shootings on the streets, in apartment doorways, and, once in the hall of his school.

Al knew that because he was accepted by neither gang, he was in danger from both. He tried to learn to protect himself. He took karate lessons at a youth center, but he was smart enough to know that the best karate moves are no match for a handgun. He thought about getting a gun himself, probably by selling his guitar to get the money. But he learned that weapons are more costly than musical instruments. Besides, he knew that he would probably never be able to shoot someone who was used to gunplay before getting killed himself.

After an especially vicious beating, which occurred after he was seen by a member of the Italian gang talking to a white girl at a street corner, he decided that for his own safety he would have to leave home.

He had no money, so he panhandled for several days on the Boston Commons to get money for food and for a bus ticket to some other place. He went to New York but got only as far as the bus station near Times Square before being beaten and robbed. Then he started hitchhiking. His grandmother had told him how dangerous this was, but he thought he had to take the chance. There was nothing for him either in Boston or New York. Someone told him that for runaways Toronto was the best place in the world. There were halfway houses for homeless kids, which the government supported, and perhaps he would be able to live there without the constant nagging fear for his life.

He managed to get to Toronto, hitching usually on trucks with his guitar over his shoulder and his clothes in a backpack he had found on a pile of discarded clothing in a New York street "where people who have more money than they need live," as he put it. He managed to get into a group home.

But the Canadian government official who inspected the home regularly found out that he was a United States citizen and, therefore, not the responsibility of the Canadians. So he was deported, right back into his old neighborhood in Boston. His grandmother did not seem delighted to see him back, although she told him that, of course, he could stay. He had to go back to school, however. And school was just as terrifying as it had been when he left, although now security guards searched students for weapons every morning before class. Still, weapons slipped through, and after a teacher was knifed in a classroom next to his, Al decided to take his chances on the road again.

This time he got as far as Los Angeles, where he was staying when I met him. He knew that there were even more violent gangs in that city than in Boston, but nobody knew of his background, and so he hoped he would not become a specific target for any group. Also, the kids with whom he lived under that overpass were of many races and colors. His best pal was Korean. He even still had his guitar, and made a few dollars playing and singing in front of restaurants and movie theaters. His songs were sad ones. "The kids tell me I'm good, and that I should try to get a job as a musician with a rock band," he said. "But that's crazy. Every other kid I meet wants to be a rock musician, and as far as I know, nobody has yet gotten into a band."

One thing that was good: The weather in Los Angeles was warmer than Boston. With a small fire or an old oil stove, the street children had managed to maintain their home under the overpass through at least one winter.

Al knew that there was no future in the kind of life he was living. He told me he would continue to look for a safe place where he could go on with his education and perhaps, just possibly, become a professional musician. There was a chance of that. His songs were really original. He sang of being "in the middle," of trying to find a place to belong. Perhaps someone would hear him and give him an opportunity to leave the streets. At least the last time

26

I saw him he had not started taking drugs or selling himself to the men in the fancy cars who cruise the area in search of young boys . . . "chickens" they call the boys. The boys call the men "chicken hawks." His worst fear was that someone would find him and return him to Boston. "It was such a hassle hitching out here," he said. "If they send me back, I'll just have to start back to Los Angeles. At least I've made some friends, and, of course, the gangs here don't seem to think I'm worth bothering with . . . since nobody else does either."

Lucinda

Lucinda wouldn't give her real name, or her age, although she looked to be about fifteen. Unlike most of the other adolescents who live in the streets, she knew exactly who and what she was. She was a dancer.

Her stage, like her home, was the street across from New York City's Lincoln Center. There, for two winters and one summer she performed dances she had choreographed for herself. Most often she used a large, portable tape player for her music. Sometimes she found street musicians to help her with her act: a guitarist, a saxophone player, or a drummer. Occasionally she put together a small band.

A small girl with straight, long black hair, she had

the figure to be a dancer. Her neck and legs were slender and long, her arms graceful. She looked as if she took excellent care of herself: There was not an extra ounce of fat on her well-exercised body; her light brown skin was flawless; her large brown eyes sparkled as she moved, sometimes fast, sometimes dreamily slow to the music she had chosen for that performance.

She would never talk much about her past . . . only about the future she hoped to have, either on Broadway or in a modern dance company. She did say that her mother (who, according to her, had died a few years before) was once a dancer, and that she was now on the street because the agency that placed her in foster families after her mother's death wasn't interested in her career plans. Her last home was with a couple who belonged to a religious sect that considered dancing immoral—"the work of the devil," Lucinda said. "They don't know what they are talking about, of course. Dancing makes you feel free. It keeps you from getting angry at the world, and it makes other people happy."

She made her own costumes, which she added to the black leotard she wore winter and summer: a ballerina skirt, a bright shawl, and red shoes. She would try anything: tap, jazz, what might be called modern dance, and, occasionally, in a pair of toe shoes, ballet. Her talent was unmistakable; her technique good enough to show that she had had excellent schooling, although to become a true professional she would have to have more formal training.

She was trying to buy what she needed with the money she collected after each dance sequence on the sidewalk. There was always a hat on the sidewalk: straw in the summer, top hat in the winter, in which bystanders could toss money. Lucinda was good enough so that a sizable number of dollar bills could be seen among the dimes, nickels, and quarters she received from her appreciative audience.

New York City has a licensing law for street performers. Lucinda didn't have a license (you need to be older and to have an address to get that, she explained), but the police generally left her alone. "That girl has guts, talent, and she's obviously staying out of trouble," one officer said. "She is not on drugs, she tells any man who tries to pick her up to get lost, and she seems to be able to manage on her own."

Among her audience there were often dancers from the two ballet companies that perform at Lincoln Center, musicians, and other artists who work in the concert halls and theaters at that cultural center. There were three outstanding schools for would-be dancers right across the street: the Juilliard School of Music, the School of American Ballet, and, probably most suitable for Lucinda, the School of Performing Arts, run by the city of New York as a public high school for gifted youngsters. Lucinda desperately wanted to get into one of those schools so that she could take regular dance class every day.

She made enough money to get the kind of food she knew she needed to keep her body in top shape. What was left over, she spent going to dance class at the various studios in the area. She said that occasionally she stole into a company class, given regularly every morning by dance companies at Lincoln Center. When she was spotted, she was, of course, told to leave. But, surprisingly enough, she managed to stay through the two-hour sessions for company members occasionally without being noticed as an outsider, she said.

After food and class were paid for, there was no money for an apartment or even a room. No one would rent her her own place anyhow, because she was too young to sign a lease, and no landlord would take a chance on renting to an underage girl who was living alone in New York. So she had fixed up a small corner for herself in one of the abandoned buildings on one of the sleaziest blocks in the city, Eighth Avenue near Times Square. There she kept her costumes, her tights, and the dancing shoes she bought at the same stores to which professional dancers go. "Shoes are the most expensive things I buy," she said. "If you get the wrong shoes, you wreck your feet. And you need good feet to be a dancer."

During the winter of 1990–1991 she suddenly disappeared. The policeman who admired her performances made an effort to find out what had become of her. Of course, he feared the worst. But actually, he found, Lucinda had, apparently, managed to take a long step toward the kind of future she dreamed of. A member of her semiregular audience, a woman lawyer, had approached her and offered to help. After much prodding, a New York City welfare agency had decided to make arrangements for her in a halfway house where she could stay until she was old enough to be on her own. That gave her an address. And she was back in school (one hoped at the School of Performing Arts) getting a high school diploma. She had also joined a regular, daily dance class, the police officer said. "It was made clear to her that she must not dance in the streets any longer, once she was taken on by that welfare agency," the policeman said. "But actually she's getting what she needs . . . the training to become a pro without the hassle of trying to find food, a bed to sleep in, a shower to stay clean, and a washing machine and dryer for her tights. That's all she wanted for the time being."

The officer said that many Lincoln Center patrons had asked about Lucinda. She had made a memorable impression on her audiences as well as on the usually unsentimental authorities, who seem unable to find a way off the streets for other homeless kids. "I expect to see her on Broadway one of these days," one dancer said. "I really think Lucinda can make it. I wonder what her real name is. She's probably too old for ballet training, but she could be a Broadway or TV dancer. She's certainly got the talent and the determination. I'd like to know what becomes of her."

Who are they, the children who run away? They are children from all levels of society whose problems seem so great at home that they come to think that "anyplace but here" has to be better. Only a few of them manage to do what Lucinda did.

CHAPTER 3

REASONS FOR LEAVING

Every one of the more than a million children and teenagers who leave home every year probably has special reasons for doing so. Those reasons are varied, as we have seen with Maggie, Al, and Lucinda. But whatever the reason is, it seems overwhelming enough that the runaway can think of no other way out. As runaways tell their stories, some of them are similar enough that experts put them into what they call "statistical categories."

This chapter gives some of those reasons. If you have thought of leaving home, perhaps your problem is like one or more of them. Some of the reasons may sound more serious than others to a person who is not caught up in the situation. However, no kid leaves home and stays in the streets for longer than a few days without feeling that anything that the uncertain future holds is better than the impossible present. In other words, again, "anyplace but here."

1. Physical Abuse   by one or both parents or by foster parents, or anyone else who has the power and the wish to inflict pain.

Paul, thirteen, is a youngster I met on the streets of Boston. He left a home where an alcoholic father hit him with belts, whips, and, once, with a wooden board. His mother was too frightened of her husband to protect her son. Paul was in the hospital several times with injuries that resulted from beatings, but his parents never took him to the same hospital or doctor twice, and insisted that his bruises, broken ribs, and black eyes were the result of accidents. While he was still living with them in a medium-sized town in Maine, nobody ever reported him as a battered child. Apparently his teachers, the doctors and nurses who saw him in emergency rooms, and his neighbors never suspected that Paul was anything but accident-prone.

After the beating with the board, Paul left. He hitchhiked to Boston, where he soon began living in an abandoned building in what the local newspapers call the Combat Zone, a dilapidated, dirty part of the city that has drug dealers at almost every corner, as well as porno theaters and shops. The residents of the area are mainly as poor and lonely as Paul. Policemen do not go alone to the Combat Zone.

At the time I spoke with him, Paul was making his living picking up men who like to have sex with young boys. He realized that he couldn't stay where

34

he was much longer. He had had sexually transmitted diseases twice already and had known enough to go to a free clinic for treatment. He did not know if he had already contracted AIDS. That disease may not show symptoms for years, and he was afraid to get tested.

Judy was fifteen when I met her. She came from an exceedingly abusive home in North Carolina. Her parents belonged to a religious sect that maintained that adults who spared the rod spoiled the child, a notion that has caused a lot of physical and psychological harm to children throughout the ages. Judy's mother believed that Judy was possessed by the devil. She thought that a girl who wanted to wear makeup, go to school dances, and behave the way most young people behave was headed straight for the flames of hell. Judy could never do anything well enough to please her parents. Whatever she did, said, or thought was considered another symptom of her sinfulness. So she was beaten regularly. Also, she was fed strong laxatives that gave her cramps and kept her out of school.

When her mother found a lipstick in her purse, she tried to force water mixed with strong soap down her throat. That's when Judy escaped, with only the clothes on her back. She headed for Atlanta where she found a district similar to Boston's Combat Zone where Paul lived. And, like Paul, she survived with the money she made as a prostitute.

35

Shortly after she came to the city, a pimp found her, befriended her, and soon, she thought, owned her. Like her parents, he beat her, but she was convinced she could not go home, and she couldn't think of anywhere else to go. Frequently she considered committing suicide. She obviously was in serious danger from emotional as well as physical illness.

According to statistics gathered by the Washington, D.C.–based Children's Defense Fund, which tries to make lives better for all American children, 1,849 youngsters in the United States are abused or seriously neglected every day in the United States.

2. Sexual Abuse can occur in school, on the playground, or in any other place where older, stronger people have the physical power or the means of enforcing their will on usually younger, weaker people. Most frequently it happens in the home, and the abuser either lives in that home too, or is a trusted relative or friend of the parents. Children and teenagers who are sexually abused often feel too ashamed and too helpless to report their situation to someone who can put a stop to it. Instead they leave.

Among the young prostitutes, male and female, on any given city street, one can find many who are there because, as one sixteen-year-old girl put it, "At least now I get paid for what I used to have to do for free."

Crystal, seventeen, had been on the streets of

36

New York at least three years when I met her. She came from just across the river, a small New Jersey town, where one might expect that her distress would have been noticed by teachers, friends of the family, or perhaps her physician. But apparently nobody did. Crystal was sexually abused by her stepfather from the time she was ten years old, within months of her mother's remarriage. "I think he married my mother so he could get to me," she said cynically. Did her mother know? "I find it difficult to believe that she did not," Crystal said. "But he made good money, and Mom had been on welfare for several years after my real dad left her. So I guess she was not ready to be on her own again." Rather than tell her mother outright or report the abuse to someone else, Crystal fled. She worried, however, that the stepfather may have turned from her to her younger sister.

Joe, fifteen, was abused by a clergyman who was also his scoutmaster. He tried to leave the scout troop, but his parents felt that he should stay. He tried to tell them what was happening, and they accused him of lying. "They thought that the reverend was a saint," he said. Of course he was deeply hurt that nobody seemed to believe him. Many parents think of abusers as perverts who stalk in the dark, finding and abducting children at random. This is not true. The vast majority of abusers are known not only to the abused child but to his or her family as well. Often they are considered to be upstanding citizens of their community who volunteer to supervise children's and teenage activities.

Joe had been so thoroughly turned off sexually by his experience that he would do anything other than become a male prostitute. So he scouted out locations for a drug dealer instead. And, to help him feel less depressed and helpless, he started snorting cocaine. Later an older addict showed him how to inject the drug into his veins. Joe was trying, when I knew him, to use clean needles (Joe, like most of the other children in the streets, knew that AIDS is spread by sharing dirty needles as well as through intimate sexual contact), but sometimes his craving became so strong he used any syringe he could get. He knew he was probably addicted. But he was sure that he could not go home. "My parents will think I'm a junkie and a bum," he said. "They didn't even believe me when I told them about that scoutmaster before I got into drugs. What would they believe now?"

3. Alcoholism and Other Substance Abuse—Parents who abuse alcohol and other addictive drugs may, while under the influence, abuse kids sexually, physically, or emotionally. Or they may simply neglect them. Among those who take to the streets, many kids come from homes where either one or both parents are so numb or so high on one or more mind-altering substances that they are incapable of taking even minimal care of their kids. When the situation

38

at home becomes too chaotic or too threatening, getting out may seem like the only way to survive. Sometimes seeing parents try to cope with feelings of stress and unhappiness with a pill or a bottle leads children to imitate this behavior and become an addict also. This becomes another reason for leaving home.

Chanel, sixteen, was a male prostitute in Los Angeles who dressed like a woman. He seemed to have almost come to believe that he *was* indeed a woman, referring to himself as "she." Both his parents were alcoholics, probably at the time he was born. By the time he was six, he was sneaking beers. "My parents didn't care just as long as it wasn't *their* beer I was sneaking," he said. "If they caught me with one of their bottles, I got beaten . . . if I took a bottle from a supermarket, they laughed and called me 'our genius.' " By the time he was twelve, he was not just shoplifting cans of beer but had graduated to bottles of vodka.

He was caught at fifteen with a bottle under his jacket by a liquor store owner and reported to the police. In juvenile court he was put on probation, but nobody really looked at his home life or suggested treatment. Apparently nobody in the court system realized that a fifteen-year-old could already be a confirmed alcoholic. To escape the probation officer as well as his parents, he ran away from his small California town to Los Angeles. He applied for various jobs, but with no identification and no home address, nobody would even bother to interview him. So he "made the best of things," as he put it, and offered himself for money to men who cruised the Hollywood strip looking for young sex partners. He continued to drink, but found that he had to take so much alcohol to get high that he got sick before he got drunk. So at the suggestion of one of his customers, he added heroin to the booze. The combination is, of course, potentially deadly.

Chanel was bright and exceedingly well-spoken. He knew perfectly well that he was in danger from a drug overdose or from AIDS, or both. But, he said, he didn't care. I got the impression that he was trying to commit suicide, although he never mentioned the word. Instead he said that he really had no future, at least none he could imagine.

4. Family Problems —Kids who run away because of relatively minor family problems like disagreements with their parents, boyfriend or girlfriend trouble, difficulties at school, etc., generally don't stay away very long. To them it becomes abundantly clear—usually within a day or so—that life on the road or on the street is much more difficult than life at home, even if that home is strife-torn.

There are, however, serious family problems that drive kids away from home on a more permanent basis. Parents who quarrel incessantly, parents who make it clear that they consider their child a dismal failure, schools that are not prepared to deal with whatever it is that makes a student unable or unwilling to get passing grades may all convince a kid to join that sad parade of street children. They have become convinced that they cannot please anybody, that they are not worth loving, and that they are, generally, misfits.

In most cases, such problems have persisted for years before the teenager turns into a runaway who stays away. Often these kids don't believe that their parents want them back (and sadly, they may be right). Many have tried to go home several times, only to find out that they are not welcome or that the problems have gotten worse. To all their other so-called faults, running away is now added to make them feel even more worthless. Often kids who leave repeatedly explain that at home everybody seems relieved when they are gone, and that a parent or some-one else has actually told them so.

Annie, sixteen, had run away from home three times. She had been on the streets of New York for about two weeks when I met her and was almost convinced that she could not survive there. She had found a job at a fast-food shop on her first day in the city (she came from a suburb), but when she could not produce a Social Security card or proof of age and other documents, she was fired. "Employers worry a lot more about hiring underage kids if they are American than if they come from some other country and don't have a green card [a government permit allowing a foreign worker to seek employment in the United States]," Annie said. She may or may not have been right about that, but she had been fired from every job she had found since she ran away from home the first time, four years before, after her parents divorced.

"When Dad first left, I thought things were going to get better," Annie said. "Mom and Dad fought constantly over everything. They spent so many nights shouting at each other that I sometimes got very little sleep. My sister and I used to pull our blankets over our heads to stop the noise. Once I even went to a drugstore and bought earplugs. They don't work too well."

But after the divorce the situation only got worse. Annie's father, by court order, took her and her sister every weekend. He would spend those weekends trying to get his daughters to spy on his ex-wife. "Why should I pay child support and alimony if she's out with other guys?" he told them. Annie was confused about that even when she was twelve. "What's my mother's dating got to do with his helping to support his kids?" she asked. "Doesn't he care about us now that Mom is no longer his wife?"

Nor was Annie's mother much more helpful. She spent most of her time bad-mouthing Annie's father and insisted that the children should choose which of their two parents they believed to be right. "How can you still care about that sleazebag?" she would ask. The first time Annie took off, it was because her mother had threatened to "make sure you never see your father again." She objected to a new dress he had bought for Annie on one of the weekend visits; her mother tore it to shreds. It was supposed to have been Annie's outfit for her first dance, and Annie was furious. Because she was angry, she was grounded. The dance took place without her. Once out of the house, she stayed away for about thirty-six hours, which she spent at a friend's house without calling her mother. When she went home, she was told that she would not be allowed to see that friend ever again.

The next time she ran away, it was because she and her sister were informed that they would be spending the next year at an aunt's house, because her mother had a new job in another city. Neither one of the girls could stand the aunt. The younger sister saw no way out . . . but Annie did. She took a bus to New York and spent three nights in the New York bus terminal until her money ran out. She was accosted repeatedly by pimps and various other shady characters and became thoroughly frightened. When her money was gone, she turned herself in to the police and was provided with bus fare home.

Living at her aunt's proved to be just as unhappy as she had expected. The aunt was much older than Annie's mother and treated her two young nieces as

43

if they were very small children. They were not allowed to visit friends after school; Annie (who by then was fifteen) was prohibited from using makeup, going to school socials or athletic events, and was told that there would be no dating until she was at least eighteen.

The aunt also made sure that the weekend visits with the father stopped. She exchanged the demand for child-support payments for his promise that he would not come near the children any longer. When he remarried and moved to another city, the girls heard about the new marriage from the aunt. He did not bother to tell them. And the aunt made it clear that their dad had no use for his daughters any longer.

"It wasn't just that she made our lives miserable . . . she kept telling us how grateful we had to be to her. She had taken us in when nobody else wanted us," Annie said, sitting with her carry bag on a bench at the New York bus station. She had used the bag for a pillow for three nights. "I just couldn't stand it anymore. Life with Aunt Margaret was pretty terrible, but I had one reason for staying. I was a member of the high school drama club, and my teacher thought I had a lot of talent. Two weeks ago I got the lead in our club's annual play. When I told Aunt Margaret, she forced me to resign from the club. 'We don't need any actresses around here,' she told me. 'Take a typing course so you can do something *respectable* when you graduate. Actresses are whores, like your father's new wife.' "

Apparently the aunt had made very little effort to find her niece. If she had, the very fact that Annie had spent three nights in the bus station might have alerted the police, who are always on the watch for runaways at bus and railroad stations. Turning herself in again would be a desperate act on Annie's part. She did not expect anything in her aunt's home to get any better. "I'd rather be a waitress in New York all my life than stay in that house for one more minute after I'm eighteen," she insisted. "I don't want to be a prostitute or a dope dealer, and those seem to be the only jobs open to teenagers. So I guess I'll go back, grit my teeth, and check the days off on my calendar until high school graduation. After that I'm off—permanently. And once I make enough money to get an apartment, I'll get my sister too."

Children who run away and stay away have good reasons for what they do. No adult would tolerate the situations in which these young people have been asked to live. Yet, no matter what they think, "any-place but here" may not be better.

CHAPTER 4

WHERE THEY GO

According to the best available statistics, a child runs away from home every twenty-six seconds. Most of these children, ranging in age from about eight to about seventeen, give up the idea of living in the streets and return home within hours, days, or weeks. For them, "anyplace but here" soon proves not to be better. But others try to survive on the streets for weeks, months, and even years. For them, there is often no place else to go—or at least that's the way it seems. Too many die before they find the better life they are seeking.

Usually those who really mean to stay away go to large cities. If they have very little money, they hitch, in spite of all the warnings they have heard about this dangerous practice. Others take buses, as it is the cheapest form of interstate transportation. A few go by rail. Most avoid planes, not only because of the expense, but because airlines keep passenger lists.

There are several reasons why large cities, especially New York and Los Angeles, attract would-be runaways. First, there is the glamour that the image of these cities projects. Anyone who has seen those "I Love New York" ads on TV sees the sparkle, the glitter, and the excitement of the city without the dangers, the loneliness, and the lack of help for those without money. The ads are meant for tourists, who come for a few days with money, traveler's checks, and credit cards—to see Broadway shows, stay in expensive hotels (the average price for a midtown hotel room is now about $175 for a night), and eat at fine restaurants (the average price for a modest meal is $20 per person). Certainly they are not meant to attract penniless teenagers who get to see none of the glamour and a great deal of the squalor, danger, and desperation under the glittery surface.

For some, especially those with ambitions to become part of the entertainment industry, the magnet is Los Angeles. Unfortunately, the story of Lana Turner, who was allegedly discovered sitting at a counter in a Hollywood drugstore, is still making the rounds. Most of today's would-be actors and actresses may never have seen Lana Turner—a star in the forties and fifties—except perhaps on late-night TV, but they have heard the story. It never was true.

Others hear similar stories about one of today's stars, for instance, Julia Roberts. Or they get the fiction of the film *Pretty Woman* mixed up with reality.

47

Many of those who work with teenage runaways hate that movie with a passion. It tells the story of a prostitute who finds a rich, attractive man. He hires her for a few nights. After a few hours, he falls in love with her, and they get married to live happily ever after. It is, of course, a fairy tale—"Cinderella" in a more up-to-date setting—but there are too many young women who believe that somehow they will meet a handsome, rich, modern-day prince, who will love them and take care of them for the rest of their lives. Whether in Los Angeles, New York, San Francisco, or Boston, a pretty teenager is much more likely to meet a pimp, who will exploit her, probably beat her up, and send her packing once she has outlived her usefulness.

Another reason why young runaways pick large cities is that they know that there they can disappear into the crowd. Getting picked up and sent back to where they came from is less likely in a city than in a small town or a rural area. "When I left, I decided a big city might be too dangerous and difficult for me, so I picked a small town in Vermont," one fourteen-year-old said. "I was picked up by the local police within two days. I had actually found a place where I thought I could live, a summer house that nobody seemed to be using. I was hoping to get a job at a fast-food joint or something like that. Then I made the mistake of going for a hamburger at one of the coffee shops on Main Street during what turned out to be school hours.

"A member of the local police force who was having lunch there at the same time looked me over carefully, and before I could get away moved to the chair next to me and started asking questions. His first one was 'Why aren't you in school?' It had never occurred to me that in a small town the police would worry about who goes to school and who doesn't. Where I come from, they have more important problems to worry about—like murder. When I told him what I thought was a good story, that I had forgotten my lunch at home and would go back to school right after I had finished my hamburger, he clearly didn't believe me. He knew right away that I did not belong in that town. He asked me a few more questions, none of which I could answer to his satisfaction, and packed me off to the nearest police station. [There was actually only one in town.] Within a few hours, I was headed back to my hometown, Hartford, Connecticut, on a bus. I got off that bus and hitched to New York. The cop had made it very clear that if he ever saw me again, I'd be off to juvenile hall, and I figured that in New York at least nobody would worry why I wasn't in school."

This particular boy had actually tried to make it on his own in a place considerably less dangerous and difficult than New York. At first glance, it seemed like a good idea. The trouble was that in small towns anyone who doesn't fit in (for instance, a fourteen-year-old who hangs out on street corners or in coffee shops during school hours) is almost immediately spotted. It's now illegal to take an adult to the end of town and tell him not to come back, as apparently the sheriffs in the Old West did with unwelcome strangers, but the situation is different if the stranger is a child. Running away from home in many states is a crime for a minor. Most suburbs and small towns don't have money in their budgets to take care of young strangers. So they do the equivalent of what the western sheriffs did: They put the child on the next bus, presumably to take him or her back to where he or she came from. Most small towns and suburbs have few welfare services for children from other cities and states, but they do have a budget for bus tickets.

A minor who refuses to answer questions may spend a few nights in the town jail and then be turned over to state juvenile authorities as an illegal runaway. And, if the state can't find a way of sending him or her back home, he or she may end up in juvenile hall, a slightly more modern term for what used to be called reform school.

The chances are, however, that a fourteen-year-old will not be picked up in New York City just for being a runaway. There the police really do have more to worry about—murder, arson, and rape. Yet the runaway in New York will find it much more difficult to get a place to stay (no empty summer houses), and hamburgers cost at least twice as much as in small towns.

A runaway may try to sleep in bus, railroad, or subway stations, only to be chased out by police, who don't care where he will go or where he came from. Sleeping on the streets is dangerous and very uncomfortable. It's apt to be very cold in the winter and very hot in the summer.

Park benches are no longer available. Small parks have fences around them and are locked up for the night. Large parks, no matter how safe during the day, have become death traps at night. Even if a runaway in the park is lucky and nobody tries to hurt him, whatever possessions he has will almost certainly be stolen. And everyone will tell him that resisting a would-be mugger can mean more than just a punch in the jaw. A knife or even a gun wound is more likely.

And what about a job that might pay for a place to live and food to eat? Nobody can legally hire a minor who does not have a Social Security card and an address. That leaves very few options, all of them outside of the law. While McDonald's won't be hiring any fourteen-year-old runaways, drug dealers and pimps will. And once minors are involved in prostitution and/or drugs, there are few ways out.

Not many agencies or individuals exist in big cities

51

to come to the rescue of a youngster in trouble. Getting picked up by the police may mean a stay in juvenile hall along with hardened youthful criminals who have been known to injure smaller, weaker fellow prisoners. After a hearing in court, a minor who has not committed a felony (that's a serious crime, such as selling drugs, burglary, or causing someone else bodily injury) may be escorted to the bus station for a trip home. Or he may be let out into the streets again, with a warning not to get into any more trouble or he might be spending years in a prison for youthful offenders. Since there are no opportunities to make an honest living, and few runaways can find a place to stay, the fourteen-year-old I met, like many others, was just where he started . . . only now he had a police record.

Also like many others, our fourteen year old started in a small town, ended up on a New York City street, went from there to juvenile hall, then was back out on the street, caught in a circle from which there seemed to be no escape.

He didn't have a home to go back to. His father had left years before, and his mother had married a man who made it clear that he did not want someone else's child around. This particular boy did finally ask for help. He went to the Salvation Army, which put him in touch with a social service agency. There a counselor tried to get his family to take him back, and when that did not succeed, the agency did not

52

put him on a bus to nowhere. Instead, they found him a group home where he could remain until he was eighteen years old, as long as he went to school, stayed off drugs, and generally behaved himself. This fourteen-year-old was at least safe, with a roof over his head and food to eat. Since he now had an address, and was going to school, he could also get a part-time job and earn a stake, so that when he was eighteen and no longer a minor, he would at least not go back out into the streets penniless. For a runaway, he was extraordinarily lucky, partly because he was willing to settle for what was possible without waiting for a fairy-tale ending.

Not all runaways are that wise or that lucky.

CHAPTER 5

THE GROUP:
NEW YORK CITY

Most young people who go to a city either live on the street, are taken in by a pimp, find some sort of shelter with money they get from helping drug dealers or selling drugs themselves, or money from selling their bodies, or, in a few cases, find some sort of shelter in a group home. But a few have created special places to live and new families for themselves. What they have done is not ideal, but it gives them a more secure life and a better chance of survival than most other runaways, at least those who have not sought some sort of adult help.

When I came to know them, six teenagers had been living together for more than two years. Their home was a section of an abandoned and condemned building a few blocks off Times Square in New York. The building was part of a New York City urban renewal project and would eventually be demolished. Two buildings in which the group had previously lived had already been torn down, and they were prepared to move when the wrecker got to their present home. They knew that there were many other condemned buildings on the same street, and, as the oldest, Sheila, age seventeen, put it, "The way this city goes, they won't get around to building anything new around here until sometime in the next century." She was probably right. There certainly would be no shortage of unsafe, boarded-up buildings scheduled for the wrecker in the distant future. And because of those buildings, these six young people had created for themselves a more stable life than most other runaways.

Sheila had come to New York alone two years before and together with five others has formed what seemed to them to be a substitute family, with its own life-style, unwritten rules, responsibilities, and even traditions. Along with just plain survival (always a problem in their lives), their main goal for the time being was to stay together. As far as they were concerned, it was them against the world.

Sheila is a street name. The street names and ages of her friends were Heather, sixteen; Tiffany, fifteen; Stretch, seventeen; Blair, sixteen; and Junior, thirteen. They would not give their real names to anyone, even though they were willing to talk about most other aspects of their lives. They distrusted all adults and most teenagers who were not in the group, and were especially suspicious of anyone who might be a

55

representative of what they call "the straights." Straight meant someone who was not homeless and probably had some authority to separate the group. That would include police (uniformed and plainclothes), representatives of the welfare department or other social agencies, fire inspectors, building inspectors, or anybody else who might turn them in and send them back to wherever they came from. And they would never tell anybody where that was either . . . just in case.

Sheila and Tiffany functioned as coheads of this particular household. It was a two-mother family, Junior said. The girls believed that they were more responsible and street smart than the boys—Stretch, Blair, and Junior—who, according to Heather, "are sometimes more trouble than they're worth, but we love them anyway."

They were what the mayor of New York, David Dinkins, calls "the gorgeous mosaic," the mixture of races and ethnic backgrounds he set up as an ideal for his city. The ideal might not work in many other places, but within the group, it apparently worked just fine.

Sheila is African American, Heather is of Irish ancestry, Tiffany's family came from Puerto Rico, Stretch is of German descent, Blair is Korean, and Junior is also African American.

The night Sheila and Tiffany met, they had been in New York for three cold, rainy days. They had no place to sleep and were both dead tired and frightened. They had come from different parts of the country, and after arriving at the New York bus terminal had found, half a block away, a fast-foot restaurant where a tolerant manager allowed them to sit down and rest . . . as long as they had enough money to buy food. But both were running short of cash.

Both also knew more about street life than many fifteen-year-old newcomers to the big city. For instance, both knew that the men who offered them a friendly ear, food, lodging, and even money were probably pimps scouting the bus station for a new crop of willing workers. They also knew enough to stay away from them.

Since the day she arrived, Tiffany had been eyeing an abandoned building one block down Eighth Avenue from the restaurant. The building was boarded up and surrounded by barbed wire, but she had discovered a way to get inside. It was dark and spooky, full of garbage and rats, with no heat, no electricity, and torn-up plumbing. Living there alone seemed more frightening than the street corner. However, living there with a friend seemed like a possibility.

The two girls decided that together they would try to spend a night there to see how things worked out. They cleaned up two rooms as best they could, found some old blankets that had been put out into the garbage by more affluent New Yorkers a few blocks farther uptown, and moved in. Within a few weeks, they were joined by the other members of the group, except Junior, who had been with them only a few months when I came to know them all.

Living together, they pooled their resources, earned a few dollars a day any way they could, scrounged for food in the alleys where some of New York's better restaurants dumped their garbage, and, if no edible garbage was available, bought their meals at fast-food restaurants. They tried not to get into trouble. The girls admitted to, occasionally, picking up men, but only if there was no other way to get money for food. Stretch and Blair had probably occasionally worked as lookouts for the drug dealers who are busy at every street intersection in the neighborhood. Of course, no one had any plans for the future . . . except to try to stay together.

Their rules were strict. Everyone shared. They all tried to help when one of "the family" was sick. Nobody talked to the police. Nobody talked to social workers or anyone else in authority either. Nobody got involved with a street gang (too dangerous), nobody got a pimp, and nobody carried a gun, although they had knives, just in case they were attacked. As long as I knew them they had remained safe from street violence, but they knew that a street artist had been shot and killed by a gang just a few blocks from their current tenement.

They tried to have fun together whenever they could. They found a Christmas tree their second

Christmas as a family, early morning. The tree had not been sold, so they took it and decorated it with whatever they could find that might look like an ornament. They had a Thanksgiving dinner made of fast-food fried chicken, biscuits, and a can of cranberry sauce they bought. They thought that they might go trick-or-treating one Halloween but were accosted by a policeman who thought that the costumes they had put together looked a little weird, and so they retreated to their "home."

They mourned together for one girl, Heather, fifteen, who had belonged to the group for a year. When she became very ill, coughing up blood regularly, Tiffany decided that she needed medical help and took her to an emergency room. The hospital decided to keep Heather, who, it turned out, had tuberculosis, a very contagious disease that most health experts thought had been almost wiped out in the United States. It has reappeared in epidemic proportions among the homeless and the poor.

When Tiffany went back to the hospital to find Heather, she was gone. Nobody would tell her what had happened to her friend. And when a nurse started asking Tiffany a lot of questions, she got out of the hospital as fast as possible. The nurse definitely could be regarded as one of the "straights," and Tiffany was not about to be detained and possibly separated from her friends.

During the winter of 1990–1991, Stretch, a tall,

painfully thin young man with rumpled blond hair and almost gray skin also started to cough. Everybody hoped that he would get well again on his own. They didn't want to risk another trip to a hospital.

Right down the street from their tenement at that time was an outreach post for an organization called Covenant House, which they knew offered homeless teenagers a shelter with warm beds, hot food, and counseling.* But they were suspicious of such organizations because they were afraid they might be reported and separated against their wishes. Actually, this was not true. Covenant House does not report runaways to the police or to any other official group. They get in touch with a youngster's family only with the specific consent of the teenager. And they can be of great help in many ways. For instance, they could get medical treatment for Stretch. But the kids would

---

*Although Covenant House was involved in a widely publicized scandal in 1989 and 1990, it is now an excellently organized and most effective source of help for teenage runaways. In many locations it is the only organization to which they can turn. The scandal involved the founder and director of Covenant House, who has left and has been replaced by a highly trained and experienced administrator and mental health professional. The board of directors has also been changed, and the financial affairs of the organization are now under expert supervision.

Covenant House is, however, a Catholic organization, and although it helps young people of all religions, it maintains the tenets of the Catholic church regarding such matters as birth control, abortion, and the use of condoms to prevent sexually transmitted diseases, including HIV.

not take a chance. Not yet. Things would have to get a lot worse before they would ask for help.

And, for the present, they were managing. The boys had brought home items left for garbage collectors in some of the better neighborhoods nearby. They had found all kinds of things that made their lives more livable: discarded chairs and a table, an old sofa, and a backyard charcoal grill. They had even acquired a small TV set. "It fell off a truck," Junior said, looking amused. Stretch had managed to tap into an electric line outside of the building, so they had lamps as well as TV, which they had attached to the local cable. Obviously, both the electric and the cable attachments were illegal, but the group worried about that only because in some way it might lead to their discovery.

Junior, the latest and youngest member of the group, was treated like everybody's child. They had picked him up when, as a shivering and frightened twelve-year-old, he was running from a pimp who sought forcibly to recruit him into his business. Junior was willing to do almost anything to survive, except to join the ranks of male child prostitutes. Even *he* had heard of AIDS.

So Tiffany and Stretch decided to hide him in their building until the pimp gave up. But they soon saw that Junior was not able to cope on his own, though he refused to allow himself to be returned to South

Carolina, where his two alcoholic parents had beat him up regularly (deep scars on his back proved that).

It was decided to keep him permanently. The group would take care of him. His assigned job was panhandling . . . no drug dealing, no sex. At this, actually, he did rather well. With his deep, dark eyes, his short curly hair, and his small delicate body, he managed to gain enough pity from tourists who visited the Times Square area to bring home about twenty dollars a night. He had become an expert at spotting those who were softhearted. Occasionally he flirted with older men looking for young boys in front of the porno theaters that dot the area. But he took off before a flirtation could become a demand for sex, usually with a few extra dollars in his pocket. The group agreed that Junior was a very talented con man.

The last I saw of them before beginning this book, the group seemed to be surviving surprisingly well. None of them could make it on the streets alone. But together they were managing. Not only were they pooling their talents and their material resources, but they also made each other feel wanted, even loved. Experts in psychology have noted often that, even under impossible conditions (concentration camps, for instance), those with support groups manage to survive somewhat better than those who try to go it alone.

The group knew that their way of life was both

illegal and dangerous. If they were caught, they could be accused of breaking and entering (they had no business sneaking into the abandoned building . . . signs closing the building, plus all those boards and that barbed wire, made that very clear). They were using electricity and cable TV for which they were not paying (the law calls that "theft of services"), and they were minors whom various state and federal laws regard as juvenile delinquents just because they have run away from home. What's more, they had engaged in activities that could send the older group members to jail, not a juvenile detention center: drug dealing and, occasionally, prostitution.

Their makeshift apartment was in violation of practically every health, safety, and fire code of the city of New York. If there were to be a fire, they would have problems getting out. The building was so unsafe structurally that it could collapse on them in a heavy storm or a deep snowfall.

What's more, that last time I saw them, another winter was coming on, and the wrecker was working two buildings away from where the group lived. They knew that their building might be coming down before it got really cold. So they worried about the future. Every once in a while one of them rang the bell at the Covenant House outreach office and peeked inside. They had talked of sending an observer to see if that organization could work out some way to get them off the streets but still keep them

63

together. Perhaps they would try to stay on their own through another winter. They just didn't know yet. And meanwhile Stretch's cough was getting worse, Tiffany had broken out in a rash, and Junior was losing weight. But Blair had found two mattresses. Junior had brought in forty dollars. Tiffany had learned that, once she was eighteen, nobody could make her go back to wherever she came from because she would no longer be a minor. And nobody really knew what could happen tomorrow. For the moment they would continue to try to face the future on their own—together.

CHAPTER 6

ANOTHER GROUP: VENICE, CALIFORNIA

Vlad, seventeen; Maria, fifteen; Debbie, sixteen; King, sixteen; Elvis, sixteen; and Blossom, fourteen, lived on the beach of Venice, California, a section of Los Angeles whose population is as mixed as the membership of this group. Venice got its name because it is built on a series of canals, like the city with the same name in Italy. Some of the homes directly on the canals or on the Pacific Ocean are large and elaborate, with boat docks in front and swimming pools in back. That's where stockbrokers, successful artists, actors, directors, or others in the motion picture and television industries live.

Some streets away from the water, however, look as if they belong to an entirely different city. The houses there are colorfully painted, but the paint is peeling. Everything looks as if someone had forgotten to do any repairs for at least fifty years. That part of Venice is known to be one of the most dangerous places in Los Angeles County. This is where the movies and TV are represented by unemployed actors, would-be directors, and struggling artists. There are also drug dealers, violent street gangs, prostitutes, and others that the people who live in the large homes hope never to meet. This is where street kids try to find abandoned or condemned homes in the winter. In the summer they live on the beach, under the boardwalk. On weekends the boardwalk is full of street artists, roller skaters, and sidewalk merchants hawking T-shirts, inexpensive jewelry, and artwork, often more notable for its bright colors than for its design qualities.

Street kids pick Venice as a place to stay because the area, like New York's Greenwich Village, is known to be tolerant of unconventional visitors. Also, the police in Venice are busy dealing with dangerous criminals and seem to have less time to cope with the underage homeless than the authorities in most other beach enclaves along the southern California coast.

Every member of the group I came to know came to Venice after having tried to live in a safer, more regulated California beach town. In Venice, most teenage runaways live in makeshift tents, constructed of materials that are easily found and replaced when, after many complaints from local citizens, the police come to tell them to move on . . . usually about once a month. But they keep coming back, putting up their cardboard-and-plastic housing on slightly different parts of the beach. Their hope is that they can disappear into the generally colorful and impermanent crowds who come to the Venice beaches to have a good time. On weekends, that's easy. On weekdays, especially cold and rainy ones, it's harder.

They tell themselves, and strangers who stop to talk to them, that, like beachcombers or surfers, their life is full of fun and romance; but it is evident to anyone who spends time with them that almost all of them are as deeply troubled, insecure, and frightened as the runaways near New York's Times Square. And, as in the Times Square area, those who have found a group to share with are better off than those who try to make it alone.

Of the group I knew, Vlad and Maria were the first who decided to occupy their particular corner of the beach; they had later been joined by the others. The couple said they were married in a ceremony across the Mexican border, and that they left their hometown near San Diego because their parents insisted that they should not see each other. They had been in love, they said, since junior high school, but Vlad came from a Russian Jewish family, and Maria, from a Mexican Catholic one. When I knew them she was five months pregnant.

"When I realized that I was going to have a baby, I knew we would have to leave," Maria said. "My parents had told me a year before that if I ever saw Vlad again, they would ship me off to my grandparents in New York. If they knew about the baby, they'd certainly do just that. Also, they would put the baby up for adoption as soon as it was born. Vlad's parents would probably send him to his uncle in Ohio, and we would never see each other again. Everybody thinks they know how to run our lives, but, if I'm old enough to have a baby, then we just have to be mature enough to be parents, and parents stay together.''

Debbie, a blue-eyed blonde, was also pregnant, but in a way less lucky than Maria. Her boyfriend disappeared as soon as he realized she was going to have a baby. She met Maria at a local free clinic where both had gone to pick up some vitamins. Neither had ever gone back for a physical examination. Neither had received any prenatal care anywhere. "They just ask too many questions," Debbie said. Actually, the kinds of free clinics that are found in some of California's large cities are known to be exceedingly careful not to drive their patients away with too much curiosity; but just because doctors need some information in order to give minimally adequate medical care, they do have to ask questions about families, medical histories, etc. Even these tactful questions were too much for Maria and Debbie, however. When they ran out of the first bottle of vitamins, they bought their next supply at a nearby supermarket.

At any rate, the two young women hit it off immediately, and Maria took Debbie "home."

King and Elvis ran away from a small Oregon town together. Both say that they were simply "different" from all the other boys in town. They were not interested in football or other sports. Both wanted to be professional musicians and hoped to join a rock band. They had tried living in Seattle, in San Francisco, and on Sunset Boulevard in Los Angeles. They had not felt secure in these places, however, and joined Vlad, Maria, and Debbie on the beach because they thought there was some safety in numbers.

Blossom, with dark brown skin, large brown eyes, and curly hair, had been with the group for only a month at the time I was there. She looked half-starved, frightened, and very sad. She said that she left her home, about ten miles away, when her mother "got engaged" after her father had left and did not return. The mother's new boyfriend made it clear that he did not want a child around. None of these teenagers believed that they could go back to their parents, and only Vlad and Maria thought that their folks were actually looking for them. The others in the group were sure that no effort had been made to find them and that, if they returned, they would simply be pushed out again.

During the summer months, life on the beach is difficult, but possible. The sun shines most of the

69

time, just as the Los Angeles chamber of commerce tells us, and, although fog and wind often roll in from the Pacific Ocean during the night and early morning hours, the teenagers can warm up and dry out during the warm, pleasant days. But in fall and winter, the beach is far less livable than it is in warmer weather.

Venice Beach also has a lot of food dealers who specialize in Oriental, Mexican, and Middle Eastern snacks along with hamburgers, fries, and franks. They give the homeless people on the beach some of the perishables they have left when night falls and the paying customers go home.

The group had been together only for the late spring and summer months when I talked with them. Nobody had the slightest idea of where to go when the weather turned cold.

Vlad, the oldest, felt a strong sense of responsibility for Maria. He knew he was going to have to find some kind of permanent shelter for them when the baby came. But he also knew that he had very little money, no medical insurance, not even a way to get to a county hospital—the only one that would agree to take Maria when she went into labor, since she had no health insurance. There is no public transportation from Venice to any of the six county hospitals in the Los Angeles area, and, of course, unlike most of the permanent residents of Los Angeles, no one in the group had a car. As a matter of fact, only Vlad was old enough to have a driver's license, even

70

if getting a car would be possible. He hoped to be able to rent one when Maria's labor pains started. What he didn't know is that most car rental agencies require either a credit card or a sizable deposit before they will let even the most dilapidated vehicle out of their lot.

Vlad had found a few temporary jobs cleaning, washing dishes, selling T-shirts, and renting roller skates and bicycles; but, like members of the New York group, he had no Social Security card or other identification. As soon as an employer came to believe that he might get into trouble for hiring a minor, Vlad got fired. He also knew that, although he could usually pick up another job during the summer, the chances of getting work during the winter, when the beaches would be deserted, were almost zero.

When Maria started to have a lot of pain and thought that she might lose the baby, Vlad, in desperation, called his parents to ask for help. He was told to come home at once . . . without Maria. "Dad swore at me and called Maria a tramp and a whore," he said. "I told them that I could not possibly leave her, and hung up before they could trace the call."

They did not even bother to call Maria's family, afraid that they would somehow trace the call and send the police.

At least Maria had Vlad to worry about her. Debbie had nobody. She knew that she was on her own, although she often asked advice about where she should go when her baby was ready to be born. When advised to go back to the free clinic, she said she'd think it over. When told that the doctors and nurses there would keep any information she gave them confidential, she did not believe that this was possible. She didn't trust any of the people whose advice she might seek. She seemed to trust only the other members of the group, who did not know how *they* were going to cope, and who had no advice or information to give her.

She also was sure that she did not want to give the baby up for adoption. "Nobody has ever really loved me," she said. "I need the baby to do that."

This is a common idea among pregnant teenagers. Many of them have felt unloved all their lives, and they think that somehow an infant will give them all the warm love and affection they have missed. They don't realize that babies are not capable of giving that kind of love. Babies must be cared for; they don't care for their mothers. Social workers call teenagers who want a child to fill up their own lives "kids with kids," and try to get the message to them that their lives will become more difficult rather than better and easier once their babies are born. But Debbie wouldn't believe that. Against all common sense, she, like many other teenagers, believed that somehow her life would start once she was a mother.

Neither she nor Maria was getting the medical attention they needed to have the best possible chance for a healthy child. Their food was stale hot dogs and hamburgers, pizza and doughnuts, obviously not the nutrition an expectant mother needs. Both Maria and Debbie thought that the vitamin pills they were taking made up for the milk, fresh fruits, and vegetables they could not afford, but any doctor would tell them that this was not so. Both were taking the risk of having a premature or low-birth-weight baby, and such infants often need months of care in special hospital nurseries if they are to survive. There is also the chance that the children of malnourished mothers may have serious birth defects, which makes it difficult to find adoptive homes for them, even if their mothers should decide that they were really too young to care for a child.

King and Elvis might also have been in need of medical attention. Both said that at times, during their stays in Seattle and San Francisco, they had injected themselves with drugs. Without realizing how dangerous the practice was, they had shared needles with other drug users. Occasionally, when there was not enough money for food, they had taken money for sex with strangers. Both had heard about AIDS, but they did not have realistic ideas about how it is spread. Both were underweight and seemed to get sick a lot. The reason for their illness might have been their unhealthy life-style, or they might have had a lowered immune response to bacteria and viruses, which could be a sign of HIV infection.

73

At the free clinic, which they had both used at Maria's suggestion, they were told that they could be tested for antibodies to HIV free of charge. They had not taken up the offer, nor had they read the pamphlets counselors gave them about HIV and AIDS. So they continued to believe that neither of them could possibly be seriously ill . . . after all, most of their symptoms didn't seem all that bad. They also refused to believe that a person can carry the AIDS virus around for years without showing any signs of illness at all, but that during all that time they can infect their sex partners. "Life is difficult enough without worrying about something that hasn't even happened yet," Elvis said when Maria urged him to get tested. But he added that he had nightmares about death.

Blossom, who said that she was part African American and part Indian, was the most helpless of the group. She was a frightened little girl who seemed even younger than her age, and who had attached herself to Vlad and Maria, pretending that they were her parents. She was terrified for fear they would go away and leave her behind. They comforted and reassured her to the best of their abilities, but they had so many problems of their own that the last thing they needed was another child to care for.

Although runaways rarely advise other runaways to go home, both urged Blossom repeatedly to call her mother. Blossom became panic-stricken when this happened. She insisted that there was no one in her family who would welcome her back. When she got upset enough, she talked about suicide. She had threatened to kill herself so often that nobody in the group took her seriously. Most experts in mental health would disagree with the group's judgment. Blossom was deeply depressed, a child who might make good her threat when Vlad and Maria decided that they had to deal with their problems alone . . . probably as the birth of their baby approached. Blossom needed counseling as badly as she needed responsible adults to care for her. When I knew her, she was seeking neither.

Actually, there are solutions to some of the problems that members of the group were experiencing. If there had been an agency or a service that would have helped them to make realistic plans, all kinds of potential disasters might have been avoided. Unfortunately, there was no such service, at least not one that would reach out to these teenagers so that they would know what kind of help might be available.

Besides medical services, Vlad and Maria, for instance, could have benefited from *legal* help. (See Chapter 9, "Minors and the Law.") They needed to know if their Mexican marriage was valid in California. It very well might be. If it was, all sorts of changes would occur immediately. If the marriage was valid, Vlad could probably be declared an emancipated minor, i.e., free of parental control. In that case, neither his family nor Maria's would probably be able to separate the couple nor take the baby away once it was born. Also, both would be eligible for assistance under Medicaid, giving them access to the medical treatment they so badly needed. After the baby was born, they would also be eligible for many different kinds of assistance, including welfare payments and food stamps, so that they might be able to find some kind of permanent place to live. Vlad could apply for a Social Security card so that he would be able to take a job legally. Both could go to school, either at night or during the day, so that they could get their high school diplomas, which would help them eventually to find better jobs. It was even possible that the baby might be able to go to day care so that Maria could finish her education.

Debbie also might have been eligible for a variety of services, including health benefits and welfare, if it could be established that she could not go home. There are group homes in California created especially for teenage mothers and their babies. The mothers are encouraged to finish high school and get some kind of job training, while their babies are cared for at the home during school hours.

King and Elvis needed medical services. If both were healthy, they, too, might have been able to stay at an agency shelter or be placed in a group home or foster care while they finished their education and got ready for jobs. If they were HIV-infected, they needed to explore the possibilities of taking AZT, a medication that is thought to retard the onset of full-blown AIDS for months and possibly for years. But to get that medication, they had to be monitored by a physician, and that meant having a permanent place to stay. The first place for them to go would have been the free clinic. They would have had to trust someone there enough to allow themselves to be helped.

Blossom needed help with her severe emotional problems. She might have had to spend some time in a mental health center or a hospital. She had to become convinced that Vlad and Maria could not care for her, and that she must find some other solution to her helplessness and loneliness. Perhaps turning herself over to a welfare department social worker would have been a good first step. There was absolutely no chance for her alone on the beach in the winter.

If they didn't get help, the members of this group would all be caught up in a crisis much worse than the one they were experiencing when I spoke with them. Maria and Debbie probably would be forced to give up their babies. No hospital would release a teenage mother and infant to the street. The chances were that, unless they made some kind of realistic plans, their infants would be turned over to the California Department of Social Welfare when they were born. In order to get the babies back, both would have to prove that they had a suitable place to live and a way of feeding and clothing the newborns in a safe and reasonably healthy environment. Blossom, if she did not seek help, would probably have been found by the police and returned to her mother, who seemed not to care what had happened to her young daughter. Once at home, Blossom would have been back on the road again within months, if not weeks, joining the runaways who are really "push-outs," and who leave home again and again. Each time they do, they become more depressed, feel more unwanted, and are less able to cope.

One hopes that something happened to allow these teenagers to reach out for help, because Venice, like so many other communities in the United States, was not about to reach out to them. Yet, like the New York group, all were better off than they would have been living alone.

CHAPTER 7

AGGIE: A SUCCESS STORY

Though most runaways find themselves living on the streets, prey to pimps, drug dealers, and whoever else finds them and takes advantage of them, a very few manage something better. The ones who do generally have no illusions about finding a glamorous life in the big city. Instead they look for ways to survive that give them shelter and food and a hope for the future. Aggie was one of those.

When I met her, she was nineteen, and for the past year she had worked as an apprentice cook in New York City. At the time she was the chief vegetable preparer in a vegetarian restaurant. Since she was a vegetarian herself and loved to cook, the job was exactly what she wanted. She also had her own apartment, a two-room tenement flat she shared with a roommate. The sixth-floor walk-up was supposed to have heat and hot water. The winter before it had had neither, but Aggie had a lease and, what's even more important, enough self-confidence to have complained to the city Department of Housing. The following September there were actually workmen in the basement, just before heat would be needed, and Aggie knew that in the coming winter she would be able to go to bed at night without wearing three sweaters, long underwear, and wool slacks. Also, she hoped the apartment would be warm enough for her to wash her short, black curly hair in her own shower instead of at the nearest YWCA.

Aggie left a violently abusive home at age fourteen and never went back. Her father was a frustrated artist who worked as a salesman, a job he hated. To make himself feel less unhappy, he drank. And when he was drunk, he beat Aggie and her mother black-and-blue. Her first memory was of herself at age two, trying to keep her father from pounding her mother's face. He hit Aggie with a chair, and she blacked out. When she woke up in a hospital emergency room, she had a concussion, and her parents told the doctor that she had fallen down a flight of stairs. They told similar stories to other hospital emergency room nurses and to various doctors while she was growing up. Of course, the stories were never true. All her injuries resulted from beatings, but her father was generally regarded as an upstanding citizen in the small town north of Syracuse, New York, where the family lived. Both he and her mother warned her that, if she told anyone of the drinking and the beatings, they would deny everything, and she would have to go to "a crazy house" because, of course, nobody would believe her.

Aggie, in spite of her miserable home life, did well in school, when she could get there. Often her home was in too much chaos for her to get to the school bus in time. There were never any clean clothes. Frequently she did not have a pair of shoes that fit her. Nobody at school seemed to notice that the tiny, pale girl was missing classes because nobody at home cared enough to get her to school. When the man who was supposed to be responsible for attendance called, her mother just told him that Aggie was "sick a lot." Actually she was, but not from any virus. Her arm was broken or her shoulder dislocated because of another attack from her drunken father.

When she entered junior high school at age twelve, she met one teacher who took a special interest in her. Aggie's father might not have had much artistic talent, but Aggie obviously did. When she managed to get to school, her drawings and paintings were usually the ones that were posted on the class bulletin board. The teacher urged her to try to come to classes more regularly. (He may have guessed what was really wrong but did nothing about it, Aggie said.) He told her that he might be able to get her a summer scholarship at an art school in Syracuse where she would be able to develop her skills and her talent. "You are good enough to get a college

81

scholarship, too," he told her. "Just hang in there."

But life at home became more and more impossible. When her father tried to add sexual abuse to the beatings on Aggie's fourteenth birthday, she packed her few belongings in a large tote bag and left, first for a friend's home in Syracuse and, when she felt she had overstayed her welcome there, for a bus to New York City.

She arrived in the city with no place to go, no money, and a pain in her hip that was later diagnosed as "traumatic arthritis." In other words, she had been beaten so often that her hip joint was permanently damaged. Arthritis is incurable.

She checked the want ads in several New York papers and found a couple who were looking for a mother's helper. With a Social Security card she had borrowed from a friend, she managed to convince the couple that she was eighteen years old, and settled into their household to clean, care for a two-year-old boy while the parents were working, cook, and generally run the household. She got paid almost nothing, but she had a roof over her head, regular meals, a washing machine and dryer to keep her clothes clean, and her employers were generally kind to her.

If it seems difficult to believe that adults would mistake a fourteen-year-old for an eighteen-year-old, one only had to look at a photograph Aggie carried of herself and the little boy. Someone took it in the park and gave it to her, she said. At nineteen she still looked very much as she had at fourteen. Her heart-shaped face had worry lines then, and it had them later. "I stopped growing when I was twelve, probably because I didn't get all that much healthy food, and I have not grown since," she explained.

She stayed in that job for a year, but when her employers moved to Washington, D.C., they did not ask her to come along. She was on her own again. She picked up a number of jobs: as a farm worker in Vermont, in a laundry in Boston, as a dishwasher in Albany, and back in New York City at day jobs cleaning apartments and night jobs cleaning offices. Meanwhile, whenever she had the chance, she continued to draw and paint. When she was not employed, she spent days in various libraries reading everything from poetry to books on the plight of the homeless. When she left school at fourteen, she already read at high school graduation level.

During the four years before her eighteenth birthday, she borrowed Social Security cards and changed her name to whatever was on the card, because that was the only way she could get jobs. She lived wherever she could: in storerooms of restaurants where she worked, in abandoned buildings with friends, and occasionally she shared a "legal" place with somebody older who was able to rent.

All the time she dreaded being caught. Her parents made no effort to find her, but she knew that if she was picked up, she would be returned to them.

Then they might make good on their pledge to have her declared mentally ill or an incorrigible delinquent. She had learned from others in her hometown that her mother eventually left her father but that she periodically returned, and that her parents were still trying to pretend that they were an average, well-adjusted couple whose "bad" daughter had run away. "What other people think matters a lot to them, and they would do anything they could to protect themselves against charges that they had abused me," she said.

The day after her eighteenth birthday she marched into the nearest Social Security office and got her own card. After that she could work under her real name. When she had a job, she was able to rent that small, dilapidated apartment. She soon took in a sixteen-year-old who was in the same spot she had been in, a girl who had had to leave home because of abuse.

And, what's most important, she was now able to plan a future for herself. She still drew and painted, and occasionally did a piece of sculpture. She still read a lot. The only piece of furniture in her flat that was actually bought at a store was a bookcase. Everything else was picked up from discards on the street, including the mattress on which she and her roommate slept.

Because she wanted to go back to school, she planned to take a high school equivalency examination. Her wide reading gave her more than adequate background for this. She was only worried about one subject: math. "I got reasonably good grades in that while I was still in school, but I haven't done much since," she said. Of course, she had to use math in her job, from figuring out measurements for recipes to doing her taxes. Aggie, homeless at fourteen, was after all, at nineteen, a tax-paying citizen.

She also had some other plans for the future. After she had passed her equivalency test, she was going to enroll in a restaurant school that had classes during the hours when she was not working. "I could become a real chef," she said. "Then I would be able to work shorter hours and could spend more time at my painting and sculpture." She had saved some money for tuition and had already been to see a bank about a student loan. Her employers were enthusiastic enough about her to be willing to cosign for a loan and to recommend her for a scholarship.

Aggie, at first glance, seemed almost unscarred by her unhappy childhood. But as I got to know her, I could see the scars: not just the physical ones, but the emotional scarring as well. She was still slow to trust anyone. Although she seemed shy and gentle, there was a great deal of anger boiling up underneath her calm exterior. One look at her drawings and paintings—which were often violent, with a lot of black and gray paint slashed across whatever she was doing—showed her inner turmoil. Once, when she was only fifteen, a close friend was stabbed to death in front of her eyes by a street gang. The subject of death, knives, and injury was a frequent theme of her paintings, even if they were not often mentioned when she talked.

On her left wrist was a tattoo of a spider, and at home she kept two tarantulas as pets in a fish tank. "I love spiders, especially poisonous ones," she said. "Tarantulas, with their orange-and-black markings and their large eyes, are beautiful. And there is one thing you can say for them that you can't for too many humans: They are not hypocrites. What you see is what you get."

CHAPTER 8

THE VANS

Though few runaways will believe it, there is help—good help—available for those willing to trust themselves to the care of others. At least, such help is available in the largest cities. The problem is that most runaways have lost the ability to believe that anyone can help them in ways that seem right to them.

The vans are gray and a little dilapidated. They leave every night about ten o'clock from two Covenant House headquarters, one in New York and one in Los Angeles. Covenant House is an organization that deals only with homeless children and adolescents—those without families, living in the streets by themselves.

From 10:00 P.M. to 6:00 A.M. the vans cruise the sleaziest parts of the two cities, carrying several hundred sandwiches, gallons of lemonade in the summer, hot chocolate in the winter, and, on a good day, mountains of chocolate chip cookies. However, even more important than the food are the driver and the one assistant: two trained, experienced social workers who are experts in talking to and trying to help homeless kids.

The night I rode with the New York van, we drove from the west side to an area near the New York docks, at night one of the most dangerous locations in the city. The driver stopped at corners where the two workers knew that kids who wanted to talk to them could find them. Sometimes one or both saw kids whom they knew, who had approached the van and received a sandwich, a drink, and some human warmth before. "It often takes months of contacts with one kid to persuade him or her that we can be trusted, and that we are able to help," said John, the driver, as he turned the van into a back alley behind a dock where a group of boys, from about age fifteen to about seventeen, were standing, waiting for customers. After a friendly hello and an offer of food, one of the boys got into the van. He was dressed like a woman: heels, a blond wig, lots of makeup, a sequined top, and a very tight skirt.

Obviously, he had met John before. The conversation went something like this:

John: "Hi . . . how are you doing?"
The boy: "Not so hot. I have this terrible cold. It won't go away. Besides, business is terrible. Last

week somebody got shot around here, and the police are all over the place. So the customers stay away."

The boy eagerly accepted the offer of food and lemonade, and sat down in the van, obviously badly in need of rest. He looked exhausted and sick. After he had been munching on his sandwich for a few minutes, several other boys joined him. All received the same welcome and asked if they could have some food too. There was a lot of general conversation about business in the neighborhood. It wasn't good, either for sex or for drugs. The recent murder of a street kid had been well publicized, and the usual number of cars cruising the area either to pick up one of the boys or to buy crack cocaine had decreased to a yearlong low, according to the first boy.

"Would you like to come in out of the cold?" John asked nobody in particular. "Would any of you like to spend some time in our emergency shelter to see if we can't find a way out of this mess for you?" The first boy indicated that he had been thinking about the possibility. "Could I wear makeup and a skirt?" he asked. "Absolutely not," John answered. "Cross dressing is out. We don't have a dress code, but I'm afraid you'll have to wear pants and stash your wig and makeup case at the door. If you want to leave, you can have the stuff back."

The boy then asked if he would have to stay in an

all-male dormitory. The answer was "Yes, for the time being." Perhaps later he could be placed with a foster family. After some consideration, the boy decided that he would not go to the shelter after all—at least not right then. "I'm scared that, with a lot of other boys, I'd get myself beaten up. They're not exactly crazy about the likes of us," he said. John indicated that nobody at Covenant House got beaten up, that there were monitors in the halls who would protect him just as they protected everyone else. "After all, around here you might get yourself killed," he said.

"I know my way around here," answered the boy, as he waved good-bye to John, the van, and the safety it offered. "I don't know my way around Covenant House." The other boys followed him back to the street corner.

John seemed a little disappointed. "I thought this time he might come in," he said. "But when it gets colder, he may still change his mind. Also, he may come if his health doesn't get better. He may have tuberculosis or be HIV positive. He ought to have a medical checkup, but obviously we can't force him to come with us. We won't even try to persuade him. Unless he makes up his own mind that he has had enough of life in the streets, there is little we can do for him, except to give him some food, along with an option to get out of this mess."

At the next stop a group of girls dressed very much

like the boy waved to John, and several got into the van. "Have you heard about that kid who got killed last week?" one of the girls asked. "I guess that means we have to find a new place to hang out. It's really getting terrible around here." Another girl pointed out that the murder victim was male. "Whoever killed him obviously wasn't interested in girls," she said.

They all got their sandwiches and lemonade, and the first girl, who said her name was Dina, asked for seconds. John checked the supplies and told her she could have another sandwich but no more lemonade. "We're beginning to run short," he told her, "and we'll obviously be around for several hours to see more kids. Once the lemonade is gone, that's all there is."

One of the girls asked about Covenant House. If she decided to seek shelter there, would she be protected from her pimp? "He saw me near the van once and he really beat me up," she said. John pointed out that the shelter doors were guarded carefully. Nobody was let into the building without an identifying pass. "No pimp has ever made it inside. . . although several stand outside and shout at us," he told her. "As long as you are with us, you'll be safe. And after we've found something more permanent than the shelter for you, your pimp won't be able to find you."

Dina asked if she had to make up her mind right that minute. "If I decide to go later, can I just get myself to Covenant House on my own?" she asked. John gave her a card with his name and the address of the shelter. "If you decide to come over tonight, just tell them I sent you," he said. She nodded. Apparently she, too, hadn't quite made up her mind to give up the life she knew, no matter how frightening, for a life about which she knew very little.

"Some of our other workers talked to Dina two nights ago, just after she'd heard about the murder," John said. "We thought she'd come with us then, but she's been disappointed so many times by adults who have befriended her and then just used her, that she finds it very hard to trust anybody. Well, perhaps tomorrow night, or next week." The other girls had also drifted away from the van, and, after waiting a few minutes to see if anybody would come back, John was on his way again.

In the course of that evening, John and the other social worker, a woman, talked to and fed several hundred street children. About thirty had taken John's card and indicated that they were thinking about getting off the street and into the shelter. Nobody had agreed to stay in the van for a ride to Covenant House, but that, the two social workers explained, is not really the main reason they cruise the dark side streets at night. "We give them the idea that they might want to come to the shelter," John said. "They mull it over, and often days after we've talked to them for the first, second, or tenth time, they appear at the door of Covenant House, alone, with the card. They may not want some of their street buddies to know that they've come to us for help, or they may still be afraid of a pimp or a drug dealer who might come after them. Or they may have checked us out before trusting us enough."

Covenant House workers tell of a fifteen-year-old boy they call Jimmy, who came to the van at 2:30 A.M. with his younger sister and half sister, asking to be picked up. "Some guy approached us, asking to have sex with me," he said. "I'll come with you, but please don't break up my family."

It turned out that Jimmy's father was dead from a drug overdose. His mother had left him and the two girls the week before. When, after several days, she did not return to their cold-water flat, they decided that they would have to find food and shelter elsewhere. They had been on the street for only a couple of nights and were scared to death.

Workers at Covenant House gave them a temporary place to stay at the shelter. A search for the mother turned up only discouraging information. She was a cocaine addict, dying of AIDS . . . and she had no ability or intention to come back and take care of her children. She could not even take care of herself.

So the kids were placed in a group home, where they could stay together, and a search was begun for a foster family willing to take all three youngsters. Until such a family was found, they would remain where they were.

Apparently, such instant rescues are rare enough that Covenant House uses this story in their fund-raising literature. Usually rescues are a lot more complicated.

For instance, while I rode in one of the Los Angeles vans, a call was received over the car phone that a fifteen-year-old girl had telephoned Covenant House over its hot line and asked for asylum immediately. She said that she had accepted a ride from a truck driver from her home, a small town south of Los Angeles, after running away from an abusive stepfather. The driver had let her off in a particularly dark and frightening part of the city, where gang violence was an every-night occurrence. The social worker at the other end of the telephone had told the girl to go to a nearby diner where he knew she would be as safe as anyone might expect to be in that part of the city. Standing on the street, she was an open target for attack. She was assured that the Covenant House van was on its way to pick her up and take her to a shelter, where she could stay long enough to sort out her immediate future.

The driver and the other worker were driving a van that had two very visible bullet holes in its side. They had been attacked in a drive-by shooting in the area of the city where the girl was supposed to be waiting for them. Nonetheless they went without hesitation, but the girl was not at the diner. They cruised the streets for half an hour, searching for her. Then they called the police to find out if she had been picked up for loitering. She hadn't. So they drove back to their garage, feeling disappointed and worried. Of course, the story might have been a hoax, but according to the woman who had taken the phone call, the girl had sounded genuinely frightened and helpless. Perhaps she had been picked up by a pimp. Perhaps she had decided that she would try to get back home on her own, or maybe she was waiting out the night in some other doorway. Perhaps she would call again in the morning. (She did not.) But since they could not find her, they also could not help her.

There are organizations like Covenant House in a number of the large cities where homeless kids wander the streets. Most don't have a national hot line. Many don't have large shelter facilities. Most are overcrowded and understaffed. Few have a nightly pick-up service. But all are a better solution for a homeless child or teenager than any street corner, probably anywhere in the world. The only problem is the fact that too few runaways are willing to accept what is there for the taking.

PART TWO

HOW TO COPE

CHAPTER 9

MINORS AND THE LAW

Laws for teenagers are different from laws for adults. Some laws that govern teenagers sometimes seem unfair. Others are helpful. And some give teenagers rights that they seldom realize they can take advantage of when they are in difficulty.

Teenagers are generally considered minors until they reach the age of eighteen. Minors can't leave home, marry, be recruited into the armed forces, or take jobs without their parents' permission. They also cannot sign legal documents (including leases or contracts) without a cosignature from a parent or guardian. On the other hand, parents, until their children have become legal adults, are responsible for the minor's living expenses and debts. There is one exception to this rule: Teenagers who can prove they are able to responsibly care for themselves and can prove that parental rights should be terminated can be declared "emancipated minors" by a court. This generally requires a hearing before a judge, who has to be convinced that there is a good reason for terminating parental rights, and the minor is indeed capable of living on his or her own. There is a chance, for instance, that Aggie, after several years of holding down jobs and caring for herself, combined with the child abuse in her home, might have been declared an emancipated minor, had she attempted to have this done.

Incidentally, not so long ago, the age when a minor turned into a legal adult was twenty-one, not eighteen. The law was changed when lawmakers, under some pressure from young people, realized that young men could be drafted at eighteen and sent off to war, when legally they were still considered children and could not even vote for the people who were deciding which wars were to be fought.

Minors are subject to a special set of laws and are judged in special courts if they break the law. Juvenile courts, which deal with minors, operate under somewhat different sets of rules than adult courts. For instance, decisions are made by judges without juries, and the public and press are barred from the courtroom. Juvenile records are usually sealed, and, even if convicted of a crime, a juvenile criminal record may not be introduced into an adult court later on. It also won't be given to the newspapers, to colleges, or to potential employers.

These special provisions are one of the reasons

many teenagers believe that nothing terrible can happen to them if they are arrested. Not so.

In the worst instances, teenagers as young as fourteen have been referred to an adult court, where they are given an adult trial for such serious charges as murder or robbery with violence. Whether or not such a charge will be tried in adult or juvenile court is up to a judge.

And, contrary to what many minors believe, even a juvenile court hearing may result in a sentence, which in many states can keep a minor locked up until he or she has reached the age of twenty-one. The sentence will be served in some kind of special detention center, many of which go by such harmless-sounding names as Green Acre School for Girls or Running Brook Camp for Boys. Actually these institutions would formerly have been called reformatories, and many are not much different from adult prisons.

What's more, some activities that are not considered illegal for adults can land a minor in juvenile court. Parents who leave home are generally not hunted down by the police unless they have left no provision for the care of their children. If a juvenile leaves home without parental permission, it is considered a breach of the law, no matter how uncaring or unloving that home really was. Also included under juvenile law are such charges as truancy, breaking a teenage curfew law (there are no curfew laws for adults unless there is an acute local emergency such as an earthquake or some other natural disaster). States may have separate laws that apply only to minors and would be found unconstitutional if applied to adults, because courts have generally found that minors are in need of special protection. Unfortunately, laws that are meant to protect can, under special circumstances, hurt, as many of the street children have found.

There are also such vague charges as "incorrigibility," "loitering," "creating a special nuisance," etc., that often apply only to minors. In Connecticut, until 1972 a girl could be arrested and sentenced to a detention center for "being in manifest danger of falling into habits of vice." Nobody seemed to know exactly what that meant. After all, no adult could possibly be arrested because the authorities thought he or she was in "manifest danger" of committing a crime—for instance, robbing a bank. Not until the bank was actually robbed would an arrest occur. Eventually the higher courts in the state found the Connecticut law unconstitutional, not because it was vague and applied only to minors, but because it applied only to females. It was stricken off the books as illegal sex discrimination.

A slightly different law that applied to both male and female juveniles was substituted in Connecticut. Similar laws already existed in most states and had been found not to violate a teenager's rights. These statutes are called P.I.N.S. laws, short for "person in need of supervision."

Often the same people who think that nothing terrible can happen to juvenile offenders because they are minors believe at the same time that these minors have no rights. Also not true. A Supreme Court decision (called *In re Gault*, in case anybody asks) provides that juveniles held in any institution against their will or convicted in juvenile court of a crime are entitled to the same rights as adults when it comes to their defense. Aggie, for instance, could have gone to her local legal aid office, if her parents had actually gone through with their threats to institutionalize her, and demanded a lawyer. Most of these legal assistance organizations are badly understaffed and underfunded, but they are obligated to provide legal services to minors if no other source of legal help is available.

Search and seizure laws that apply to adults also apply to juveniles. That means a minor's room or person cannot be searched without the minor's permission (or, under special circumstances, the parents'), unless the police officer has a warrant. There is one clear exception to that rule: If the juvenile is caught in the commission of a crime, even if that crime is unrelated to whatever it is that the police are searching for, he or she may be searched without a warrant. That includes the place where the juvenile lives, his or her car, school locker, and so on.

This, of course, puts teenage runaways in a position where they and their possessions can almost routinely be searched without a warrant. Take the members of the group living in the abandoned building as an example. They were guilty of several offenses, including running away from home, breaking and entering (the unoccupied building in which they live), attaching wires to electrical lines (theft of services), and probably a few other charges a policeman would think of as he viewed their life-style. So they could be stopped, searched, and their living quarters could be searched for drugs, stolen goods, or other items without a warrant.

But they, like the children who live in middle-class homes with their parents, are entitled to the services of a lawyer once they are arrested. Few of the street children interviewed for this book knew this vital fact. Nor did they know how to find a lawyer if they needed one.

Again, most cities have some kind of legal aid or legal assistance office. These offices can be found in the white pages of the phone book under their correct names, or in the yellow pages under Legal Aid. If there is no such listing, the city or county bar association will give information about free legal services for children and teenagers. Just asking for a lawyer may get a court case derailed or thrown out after a conviction if no lawyer is available. The moral of this story for any minor is: When in legal trouble, ask for a lawyer. Find one on your own if you can. If you can't, make sure that your wish to consult one is noted. And realize that if you are accused of an offense serious enough to land you in detention, you do not have to answer any questions without a lawyer present, and you are also entitled to have a lawyer at a juvenile court hearing.

So, when in doubt, every minor should ask for a lawyer, even if they know they are innocent of any crime. Laws are too complicated to deal with on one's own. That's why law school takes three years after college graduation.

CHAPTER 10

STAYING AT HOME BASE: HELP WITH SEXUAL OR OTHER PHYSICAL ABUSE

Whenever a situation becomes unbearable, one's instinct is to run. This is as true for animals as it is for humans: Nature has built a sense of self-protection into all creatures, and removing oneself from a dangerous spot is a very natural way to act. But what is natural is often not sensible. Most human problems, even those that seem most threatening, can usually be dealt with best from home base. Whether the crisis that drives a teenager to pack up a few belongings and to flee into an unknown future is a violent, alcoholic father, or a sexually abusive uncle or cousin or brother, or whatever, it's usually easier to find help in one's own territory than on some strange city street corner.

Often, however, it takes even more courage to try to solve the situation at home than to run away from it. When a child is abused by someone whom he or she is supposed to love and trust, and who is supposed to love and care for him or her, the blow to self-esteem is serious. Some adult women become battered wives because they feel too helpless and hopeless to leave their husbands. The abuser always makes sure that the victim feels responsible for the abuse by letting her or him know that it was that person's "badness" that caused the abuse in the first place. If an adult can eventually come to believe this, it is no wonder so many children and teenagers do.

A person with low self-esteem finds it difficult to believe anyone can care about his or her situation, so abuse victims frequently allow their situation to continue until they become truly desperate. They may even fear for their lives. For battered women, shelters are now provided, with secret locations so that the battering husband will not be able to find them. Unfortunately, no such facilities are immediately available to battered children. (Work on this book has convinced me that there should be one in every town and city.)

Then there is the fear that nobody will believe a story of assault and battery by a father who may be a highly respected member of the community, or even by a teacher or employer. Again, many adult women do not report rapes because they are convinced they will not be believed, especially if the rapist is someone they know. So it is no wonder that someone like Debbie, who was sexually abused, or Aggie, who was battered by her father, take to the road instead of reporting what is happening and asking for help to get out of the house, if not out of town.

There was indeed a time when few people believed that a parent or some other close relative would physically or sexually abuse a child. That has changed drastically within the past few years. Celebrities like Oprah Winfrey and Roseanne Barr Arnold have talked openly about their abused childhoods. So have other very prominent women like Florida's former U.S. senator Paula Hawkins. Authorities who used to discount complaints from children as a fantasy now listen and investigate. Indeed, in almost all states, any complaint to a social worker, a doctor, a teacher, or the police must be reported to child welfare authorities immediately and followed up with a thorough investigation, after which action is taken to get the threatened minor out of the dangerous household as quickly as possible. The complainant, under law, must always be given the benefit of the doubt.

If, as was the case with Maggie—who found enough courage to report to a welfare worker the fact that she was being sexually abused and otherwise exploited in her foster home—the person to whom the abuse is reported does not listen, the teenager should find someone else in whom to confide. This is often exceedingly difficult to do. After all, not being believed adds yet another layer of abuse to what has already happened. However, if Maggie had told

108

her story to a teacher, or even called the 800 number child abuse hot line,* there is every chance that the welfare worker who ignored her would have been reprimanded or even fired. If Maggie had been able to work up enough courage to continue her search for help a few days longer, she would, in the end, have not only received the assistance and support she needed for herself, but she might even have helped other children in similar situations to get the assistance *they* needed. The chances are that the welfare worker who refused to believe Maggie had acted in a similar way to complaints from other sexually abused kids. She was obviously in the wrong job and needed to be replaced by someone who had enough sensitivity and enough training to save the children entrusted to her care.

What's more, any information that Maggie gave to a professional would have been held in the strictest confidence. If she wished, the investigation would have been followed up without indicating to anyone that *she* had been the one who brought it to the attention of the authorities. Her foster parents would simply have been told that *somebody* had reported child abuse, and that the report was solid enough to warrant a complete investigation. If the foster parents refused to answer questions, they would have immediately lost their certification to care for homeless

---

*Hot line numbers are listed at the end of this chapter.

kids. Meanwhile, Maggie would have been removed from the home even before any questions were asked.

Even after her accusation had been found to be true, and the couple and the neighbor who raped her had been arrested and taken to court, it would have been up to Maggie to decide whether or not she wanted to testify against them. One would hope that she would.

If Aggie was too embarrassed about her abuse to confide in her teacher, she, too, could have called the child abuse hot line 800 number, although getting her out of that dangerous home might have taken a little longer. The hotline gets in touch with welfare authorities in the child's state, and that route, except in the case of sexual abuse (when everybody gets indignant enough to take prompt action), might have taken longer. Hot lines are not at home base . . . they have to get in touch with someone there. So even when reporting abuse, the best route is the shortest, and that is almost always an agency in the town or city where the abuse took place.

Aggie was one of those victims who was convinced by her family that she was the "bad" one—that she probably deserved what she was getting. Her mother refused to take seriously the beatings her daughter was receiving. Everybody was afraid that the father, who, in spite of his drinking, still brought home a paycheck, might be jailed if the beatings were exposed. So Aggie was too intimidated and felt too hopeless to try to deal with her problem at home. But at least she did not run to an unknown destination. She went to Syracuse to stay with a friend. And she always found a place to stay in the many years she was a teenage runaway. If she had to spend a few days on the street, she spent those days looking for a more permanent home. That's one of the reasons why Aggie's story had a happier ending than Maggie's.

Lucinda, the dancer, left home for a purpose: She wanted to get the training to become a true professional. Her methods were at best chancy. If by sheer good luck she had not been "discovered" by the lawyer who helped her, she would probably still be dancing in the streets, and she might have drifted into the kind of life that Maggie is forced to lead. But, in spite of all her problems, Lucinda always planned her next step. She found the one place where her abilities might produce some future training as well as enough money to live on: Lincoln Center, where dancers and dance lovers gather almost every night. She made sure that she got adequate nutrition, kept clean, and took whatever classes she could in order to prepare herself for dancing on a stage instead of a street corner. So, in a way, she made her own luck, something that will never happen to Maggie.

The teenager who found the most practical solution to his problem was, of course, Don, the boy who spent several years at my house. When he left because he could no longer put up with his father's beatings, he first went to live in an empty summer cottage with friends, in his hometown. When he got into serious trouble, which might have landed him in a juvenile jail, he turned to the parents of a friend to ask for help. If he had not been able to make his home there, he would most probably have found some other adults who were willing to take him in. He was able to do this because he never even considered taking off for an unknown destination. Instead, he never went farther than five miles away from his home base.

National Hot Lines

Childhelp USA (child abuse and domestic
violence hot line)   1-800-422-4453

Covenant House Nineline   1-800-999-9999

National Domestic Violence Hotline
Helps battered women find shelter   1-800-432-9777

NOTE: All national hot lines can be called free of charge.

Local Telephone Numbers

Call any family service agency affiliated with Family Service America. Look in the yellow pages of a phone book under Family Counseling or Family Services, or look in the white pages under Family Service of (name of city or county).

CHAPTER 11

STAYING AT HOME BASE: HELP FOR UNPLANNED PREGNANCY

Vlad and Maria ran away from home when she thought that she was pregnant. Both were afraid that their families would separate them and that Maria would be forced to give up her baby as soon as it was born. Although she certainly had not planned to have a baby before she and Vlad could afford to get married, she was also not about to give up the child for adoption. So both ended up in a makeshift disposable shelter on a beach in California. Neither had a job nor the kind of education that is required to get steady employment above the minimum-wage level, so they did not have a chance of establishing a permanent home for themselves or their child.

Maria was getting no prenatal care and did not

even know how to find a hospital that would agree to take her in when the time came for the baby to be born. She was also not receiving the kind of nutrition that she needed to have a healthy baby.

Teenagers like Maria and their infants are at much higher risk for disease and complications than young women who get adequate prenatal care and have their babies in a hospital under the supervision of a physician or midwife who has seen them during their nine months' pregnancy. Maria's future health, even her life, might be in danger because she and Vlad would be unable to respond to an emergency such as a sudden rise in her blood pressure, medically known as hypertension. Hypertension in pregnant women often results in toxemia, which brings on a premature birth. Or, at worst it can cause eclampsia, which can kill both mother and baby. Maria also did not know whether or not she had diabetes or any number of other conditions that could affect her own health and that of her baby. At the beach in Venice, she would almost certainly not get to medical attention in time, should she be confronted by a major health crisis.

She had told herself and a worried Vlad that in the old days women living on the prairie or riding on wagon trains just had their babies wherever they happened to be when labor started. The story that a woman would just stop plowing the fields or milking the cows long enough to give birth to an infant has circulated among pregnant teenagers for generations.

114

After all, they tell themselves, having a baby is a perfectly normal affair. Only in modern times have women seen doctors and gone to hospitals for the birthing process.

What Maria didn't know, and neither do most teenage mothers, was that in those idyllic-sounding old days the infant mortality rate was, in some places, higher than 50 percent. Maternal mortality rates were also exceedingly high. All one has to do is go to cemeteries in some of those old prairie towns. There one can find hundreds of little graves with stones indicating that the baby whose name is on the stone died at birth or very soon thereafter. There are also a considerable number of gravestones in memory of young women who died in childbirth.

Actually, in those old days there was not really very much medicine could do to prevent these deaths. Today almost all pregnancy-related deaths are un-necessary, and in countries where prenatal care is a matter of routine, infant mortality rates are much lower than those in the United States. In infant mor-tality rates, the United States now ranks twenty-sixth, higher than many developing countries, and certainly higher than *all* European democracies or Japan. Many of those deaths occur when teenage mothers without prenatal care have unplanned babies.

In addition, even if Maria could find a hospital bed just before her child was born, there was no chance that the hospital would let her leave with the

115

baby if she had no place to call home and no way to provide even a minimally healthy environment for her newborn child.

As we have already indicated, if a teenage girl delivers a baby without the ability to care for it after birth, the hospital almost always notifies the local health department and/or the state department of social services, for exactly the same reason that a social worker or doctor who suspects that a child has been abused has to notify authorities. Having a baby and placing it in serious danger after birth is, correctly, considered child abuse, even though the parents love the child and want to keep him or her.

When Maria suspected that she might be pregnant, she, too, should have sought help at home base. First, she would have been given a pregnancy test. There is a chance that she was not pregnant at all, even though she had some of the symptoms. Then she would have been given a thorough physical to make sure that she was healthy enough to produce a healthy child. Any physical problems would have been treated promptly. Since she was sure that she and Vlad wanted to have the baby, terminating the pregnancy would not have been an option, but, if she had had doubts, she could have talked over the entire situation with a trained, experienced counselor and made plans for her future and that of her child. Since Vlad loved Maria and wanted to be involved in her life and that of their baby, he would have been made a part of this entire process, just as if the couple had been married.

If Maria had gone to a clinic or a family service agency with her problem, she would also have received advice on her legal rights, i.e., that her family could not force her to give up a baby unless she agreed. She would have received advice on what kinds of benefits she could expect from government programs for expectant mothers and their babies. For someone in Maria's situation, running was the worst possible decision, no matter how angry and threatening her parents and Vlad's family would have been had they found out that the couple was expecting a child.

For any long-term extensive counseling, a family service agency would probably have insisted that the families be included in the sessions. The agency would be risking a lawsuit from either family if they did not inform them that they were working with two minors. But it is also possible that with the help of a counselor who had worked with hundreds of couples like Vlad and Maria, either or both families might have been persuaded to accept the situation and to help the couple make the best of it.

Another source of help would have been the nearest clinic run by Planned Parenthood. There Maria could have received her medical tests, prenatal care, and a referral to an appropriate hospital to have her baby. She might also have been given abortion counseling if she asked for it. Planned Parenthood does

117

some family counseling but does not have the staff to provide the kind of help with emotional and social issues that a family service agency can. On the other hand, Family Service would not be able to provide the medical assistance. So a combination of the two agencies would have been an almost ideal solution to Vlad and Maria's problems.

If Maria were entirely sure that she did not want to terminate the pregnancy, she might also have sought help from Birthright, an organization whose primary function seems to be to persuade young women to avoid abortions. Birthright, in most communities, does not run clinics or provide medical service. They do, however, refer pregnant women to hospitals and physicians. Usually the counselor at a Birthright office is not a medical professional or a trained social worker. The counselor may be a volunteer, trained by a Birthright professional. Some Birthright affiliates may also give the pregnant woman, free of charge, clothes and diapers for the new baby.

If Maria had been considering adoption, a family service agency counselor would probably also have been the best person for her to see. The counselor would not try to persuade her to follow any one course, but would help her to sort out her options. A pregnant teenager who has not yet made up her mind about what she wants to do, and who may be under considerable pressure from family and friends to give up the baby or, for that matter, to keep it, needs this kind of help to make sure that the decision she makes is one with which she feels really comfortable.

In some communities, family service agencies also work out adoption arrangements. In others they don't but are able to refer their clients to the best possible adoption agency in their own communities.

If Maria decided to have her baby away from her family, there are maternity homes where she could go from about her sixth month of pregnancy until after she had recovered from childbirth. Some of these homes have religious affiliations, others do not. Many are part of adoption agencies and assume that the baby will be available for immediate placement after it is born. But even such a home cannot take the baby against the mother's will, even if she is a minor. However, pregnant women should try to avoid homes affiliated with adoption agencies if they have not yet made up their own minds as to what to do. The pressures from such an agency right after childbirth, when a young woman is most vulnerable and feels most helpless, can point her in a direction she may later regret. It's also important to know that in most states she will have a chance to change her mind about adoption for weeks, or even months, after the birth, depending on state law. Any woman, even one who is sure before the birth that she wants to have her baby adopted, should ask what, in her state, that time period is.

The worst decision anyone can make is to turn the baby over to an unlicensed baby broker. Such an individual may be a lawyer, a nurse, or even a doctor. He or she usually charges a hefty fee to the adoptive parents, which may be called a "fee for professional services." Also, the birth mother may be paid for giving up the baby, usually by having all her medical expenses paid, plus a lump sum when she signs the infant over. However, often baby brokers will give the newborn to the highest bidder with not much investigation as to whether or not the would-be adoptive parents are suitable. To make sure that the baby has the best possible home, a licensed agency—which can usually have its pick of hundreds of couples for every baby and can thoroughly investigate each couple's emotional stability, real love of children, financial responsibility and other important factors—is one way to insure the baby's future and put the birth mother's mind at rest.

There are no hot lines specifically for teenagers with unplanned pregnancies.

Local Telephone Numbers

Call any family service agency affiliated with Family Service America. Look in the yellow pages of a phone book under Family Counseling or Family Services, or look in the white pages under Family Service of (name of city or county).

Planned Parenthood

Look in the white pages of the phone book under Planned Parenthood.

Birthright

Look in the white pages under Birthright. In some states, there is also a toll-free 800 number. Call the operator at 1-800-555-1212 for the Birthright toll-free number.

CHAPTER 12

STAYING AT HOME BASE: PROBLEMS WITH FAMILY, SCHOOL, FRIENDS, AND WITH ONESELF

Recently, on her afternoon talk show, Oprah Winfrey turned to her audience, mainly made up of adults, and asked, "How many of you think that you grew up in dysfunctional families?" About one thousand audience members raised their hands. "How many of you came from families you considered happy?" Winfrey asked next. The impression was that about ten audience members raised their hands. Apparently the vast majority of those who attended the talk-show taping felt that their parental homes were neither happy nor well adjusted. *Dysfunctional* is a relatively new popular-psychology term meaning unhappy, not working right, just plain unsatisfactory in some way. Judging from that TV show, which seems to draw a fairly representative audience in the Chicago area, along with newspaper articles, other TV shows, and a whole spate of best-selling personal advice books, a large number of adults in this country seem to think that their home life, with their parental families, was less than ideal. Yet most of those same adults believe that they are getting along just fine with their own kids.

Probably if a TV host asked an audience of teenagers if their families were dysfunctional (after, of course, explaining what was meant by the term), the response would be about the same as it was with Winfrey's audience. Actually, what this means is not that most parents are doing a poor job. It simply means that there probably is no such thing as an ideal family, except perhaps on a few TV sitcoms ("The Cosby Show" comes to mind), and some of those old-fashioned—and one hopes no longer used—grammar school textbooks about Dick, Jane, and Spot.

Very few adolescents are completely satisfied with their parents and their home. In fact, most mental health experts agree that a certain amount of rebellion is normal for teenagers. In order to make the necessary separation from parents, in order to become their own person, children have to test out their own ideas and ideals, even if these are in disagreement with some of those held by parents, teachers, and other authority figures.

123

If most kids have some criticism of their home life, very few run away from home for that reason. Most of the hundreds of runaways interviewed for this book had much more serious problems. They suffered severe abuse, or their families had disintegrated, or they were pushed out by parents and relatives who were too unhappy or too mentally and emotionally ill to be able to care for their children. Those who ran away as a symptom of rebellion or to try to scare their parents into being more cooperative, or for some other reason than that they feared for their lives, their health, or their ability to stay sane in an impossible environment, generally returned rather quickly. A few who left for reasons that, on thinking the situation over, did not seem important enough to warrant the dangers and discomforts of a street life, sometimes got into serious trouble before they had a chance to go home. Indeed, that is one of the main considerations anyone who is even thinking of leaving would want to ponder.

Family problems that are short of life- or health-threatening are certainly better dealt with at home base. Anyone who considers his or her parents unreasonable, too strict, old-fashioned, nontrusting, prejudiced, or too demanding might want to first ask, "Do I *really* believe that my parents are acting in the way they do because they don't love me?" With all that talk about dysfunctional families, the truly important question is just that. If there is love in the home, most other problems tend to involve simply a failure to communicate, an inability to talk over disagreements rationally and to sort out options that might lead to solutions acceptable to everybody. Anybody who looks for an ideal situation, either at home or on the street, is bound to be disappointed. Indeed, the street may make even a home that is far from ideal seem just great.

The kinds of problems that most kids have with parents can be dealt with through the kind of professional counseling that is available in almost every community. It may seem difficult to confide one's worries and conflicts to others. It's also difficult to admit that one feels isolated, anxious, or depressed in a country where being happy is considered not an exception but the rule and a sign of virtue besides. But the fact is that most people, including adults, are not completely happy most of the time. Parents, like their teenage children, are often confused, anxious, and unsure of themselves. Many are afraid that, if they put their foot down, their kids won't love them anymore. Others feel that if they show too much affection, they will lose their children's respect. For all of these misunderstandings and difficulties, professional help can work wonders.

There are teenagers who give as a reason for leaving "I thought I was going crazy—that's why I ran." Many of these can't quite put their finger on what was driving them "crazy." Sometimes there may be an unresolved conflict at home. Sometimes there may be a physical or psychological cause that can be dealt with under medical treatment. Whatever the reason, however, anyone who feels unhinged at home will almost certainly feel more disjointed, more alone, more helpless, more anxious, and more depressed—in other words, crazier—on a street corner in a strange town.

An adolescent who goes to a school that has a guidance counselor or a school social worker on its staff is lucky. That's the first resource he or she should seek out. These professionals, who are trained and experienced in dealing with adolescent and family problems, often can bring parents and children together for productive discussions that seemed impossible at home. With a third party to mediate, to explain the differing viewpoints to all concerned, and, most of all, to suggest options that nobody in the family might have thought of before, solutions can sometimes be reached.

Remember all those news stories you hear about actions that are taken by school boards and colleges when some kind of severe crisis strikes? Whether it is a natural disaster like an earthquake, or a large fire, or a man-made occurrence like a mass murder or a series of teenage suicides, the first announcement is usually that "crisis counselors" will be brought in to help young people deal with the tragedy. The counselors are social workers, psychologists, psychiatrists, and other mental health specialists. In some communities, these same counselors are available at other times, only nobody thinks of asking them to come to schools to reach out to individual teenagers who might be in less-than-sensational kinds of trouble. Often the young people have to find them on their own.

This may seem like a lot to expect from a troubled kid. But those who are wise enough and courageous enough to seek their own sources of help find that it's by far the best way to handle almost any kind of trouble.

If there is no social worker or guidance counselor in the school, there is often a school nurse. She may know where other helpful professionals can be found. They may be part of the school system but located in another building somewhere else in town. Or they may be in the local mental health center, or the family service agency, or a child guidance clinic. Incidentally, child guidance clinics don't just deal with little kids: Many of their clients are teenagers and their families.

There are some clergymen, scout leaders, professionals at boys' and girls' clubs, and others who can serve as counselors for troubled kids and as mediators with parents. Teenagers often sense who can be trusted to be truly concerned, and who will simply preach at them, blame them, refuse to listen to them, and generally make them feel worse.

Professional social workers, psychologists, and guidance counselors are usually able to keep completely confidential whatever anyone who comes to

127

them for help tells them. They will not discuss what is told them with parents or other authority figures without permission, unless there is a threat of suicide, harm to a third person, or some other overwhelming reason. In a few states, confidentiality is a matter of law. In others, it's a matter of professional ethics.

Other very good sources of help are so-called support groups. There are support groups for children who worry that they might be addicted to alcohol or some other kind of drug, those whose parents, brothers or sisters, or even friends seem to be addicted, those who come from homes where there has been a divorce or a death, those living with stepparents to whom they find it difficult to relate, and many other kinds of problems. Indeed, these days there are so many support groups that some kids belong to more than one because they have more than one problem. The groups are usually organized by such agencies as Alcoholics Anonymous, drug councils in various communities, family service agencies, and other community organizations seeking to help troubled teenagers. These groups help because they tend to make their members feel less alone with their specific problem, and because the members can share experiences and ways to cope. Children with problems may find it difficult to discuss them because they are frightened or ashamed or because they feel that they are the only people in the whole world who have these particular problems. Often just knowing that there are many others in the same boat can give a troubled person a great deal of relief, and show him or her the way to take the first step in improving their situation.

Here are some national hot lines and a few local resources that may help with specific problems:

For family problems, call your local board of education and ask whether there are school guidance counselors, school social workers, or psychiatric or psychological consultants available in your school system. If there are, make an appointment.

Call your local family service agency, affiliated with Family Service America, and ask to speak to a social worker. Outline your problem and ask if you can make an appointment. An agency will probably see a troubled teenager *once* without family members present. After that, family will have to be involved. If the teenager wishes, the social worker will call the parents to set up further counseling sessions.

Child guidance clinics may work independently or be part of a local mental health center or medical school department of psychiatry. Look in the white pages under Child Guidance Clinic of (name of town or county). Sometimes these clinics are listed in the yellow pages under Mental Health Services. Child guidance clinics are staffed by psychiatrists, psychologists, and social workers with specialized training in helping children, teenagers, and families. Usually, would-be clients who are minors are not seen without parental knowledge or consent. However, the clinic may volunteer to call the parent to make an appointment, indicating that the teenager has approached them first.

National Hot Lines

Helpline/National Institute on Drug Abuse
                                    1-800-662-HELP
Provides information on all kinds of drug abuse and referrals for crisis intervention and treatment for substance abusers and their families.

800 COCAINE   1-800-COCAINE

Provides information and referrals on all kinds of drug abuse, not just cocaine.

Local Telephone Numbers

Alcoholics Anonymous/Al-Anon/Alateen

Look in the white pages of a phone book under Alcoholics Anonymous or Al-Anon. Provide information on alcohol-related problems and support groups for adults and teenagers. Alcoholics Anonymous is especially for those who recognize that they have a drinking problem. Al-Anon and Alateen are for those who have to deal with problem drinkers in their families.

CHAPTER 13

AT HOME OR ON THE ROAD: AIDS

In November of 1991, the Centers for Disease Control, the government agency in the United States that keeps track of who is healthy and who is not, estimated that anywhere between one million and one-and-a-half million people in the United States were already infected with the human immunodeficiency virus (HIV). HIV infects and destroys the T cells in our blood, which are a key part of our immune system. A person who is infected with HIV is infected for life. Although in the beginning there may be no symptoms, eventually the infection leads to a deadly series of complications known as AIDS. There is no cure for AIDS.

Reporters don't generally make very good statisticians. But just by guesswork and instinct, it seems that the vast majority of teenagers who were interviewed for this book had put themselves in serious danger of contracting AIDS, and almost all of them were convinced that they could not get the deadly disease. They gave all kinds of reasons: "I am too young." . . . "I am too healthy." . . . "I am not gay." . . . "Women don't get AIDS." . . . "I use some kind of protective lotion or cream when I have sex." . . . "I don't have sex with people who look as if they had AIDS." The reasons were endless—and they were all wrong. Even kids who already had early symptoms—hacking coughs, frequent fevers, sudden weight loss, sudden exhaustion—insisted that they just had some kind of flu bug, or that they were simply run-down.

Then something happened: American sports hero Magic Johnson got on television and announced that he would have to retire from basketball because he had been infected with HIV. He added that he had been "naive" about AIDS. "Here I am saying it can happen to anybody, even me, Magic Johnson," he said, standing in front of what looked like more than one hundred microphones, all six foot six of him, and looking like the healthiest man in the world.

Johnson said he was not gay, nor had he had any homosexual contacts. He did not take drugs. Just two months before, he had been married, and his wife was now pregnant. He obviously had not known that he was sick. His infection had been diagnosed with a blood test that was part of a routine insurance examination. Minutes after his announcement, AIDS hotlines lit up all over the country. Health department and clinic telephones began to ring. Apparently hundreds of thousands of people who had believed that they could not possibly be infected with HIV or get AIDS suddenly realized that maybe if Johnson could be sick, so could they.

One can only hope that among those who got on the telephone and made an appointment for the simple HIV-antibody test were some of the teenagers who had insisted, after repeated reminders from adults that they had exposed themselves, that they could not get sick: Beau and Jennifer and King and Elvis and Maggie and Aggie and Al—all the kids whom the experts call "at risk."

By November of 1991 more than 196,000 cases of full-blown AIDS (the series of deadly diseases that can occur when the immune system has been destroyed by HIV) had been diagnosed in the United States alone. Sixty-five percent of these had already died.

Although the first cases were discovered in gay men, the virus has long since spread to all segments of society: to heterosexuals, both men and women, and to infants, who acquire the infection in their mothers' womb or when breast-feeding.

On one hand, AIDS is exceedingly infectious, and on the other hand, one has to almost go out of one's way to be exposed to it. It can only be transmitted

133

through the exchange of certain body fluids, specifically blood, semen, vaginal secretions, and breast milk. A man can get it from a woman, but that seems to happen more infrequently unless a man has a cut or an open sore on his genitals. Nevertheless, that is apparently the way Magic Johnson got infected, so one has to be careful in any kind of sexual contact.

One way to decrease the chance of getting AIDS is *always to use a latex condom* during intercourse and oral sex. That's called by some safer sex, although even this kind of sexual behavior is not completely safe. *Only abstinence is truly safe.* Condoms are not 100 percent foolproof: They have been known to tear, to contain manufacturing defects, or to have been on the shelf, in the nightstand drawer, or in someone's pocket so long that the latex has deteriorated. Incidentally, there are many kinds of condoms not made of latex. These are no help at all. The material is too porous and allows HIV to seep through.

Another way people acquire HIV is by injecting themselves with drugs that are mixed with infected blood. Many who experiment with illegal drugs exchange needles (almost all the teenage drug users in the street do), and HIV gets into the bloodstream right along with the drug. Washing the needle with soap and water is no good, even if boiling water is used. The one substance that will help to disinfect is Clorox mixed with water, but even that is not 100 percent effective.

The truly terrifying fact about this disease is that it has been spreading more rapidly through teenage populations in major cities than any other section of the population. Most of the teenagers who contract it are not gay, generally healthy, and completely convinced that there is no way they are going to get sick. Usually it never even occurs to them to get tested before the symptoms of advanced disease (pneumonia, a certain kind of cancer, brain infections, and others) have become obvious. During the period when they are infected but have no symptoms—or the kinds of symptoms that look like a standard case of flu—they can, however, infect others, including unborn babies.

It is therefore terribly important that anybody who has engaged in what experts call "at risk" behavior get tested, the sooner the better. In the first place, although AIDS is incurable, its worst effects can sometimes be postponed for years with new medications. However, the medication should be started early, usually before serious symptoms have set in, to be most effective. Magic Johnson began treatment with the most widely used medicine, AZT, immediately after his HIV infection was discovered. The second reason is that, even without any symptoms, a person who is infected with the virus can transmit it to others through unprotected sex or by sharing drug needles.

Since the very idea of AIDS tends to produce

panic among those who don't know how it is transmitted, it is also important to emphasize that it cannot
be caught through what most people refer to as casual
contact. You can't get AIDS from hugging someone,
from shaking hands, from sharing food, from living
in the same apartment, from a cough or a sneeze, or
from any of the other activities in which one would
engage as part of everyday life. Parents and foster
parents who regularly change the diapers of AIDS-
infected babies have, as far as the Centers for Disease
Control can discover, *never* acquired the infection.
Health professionals who take care of AIDS patients
have become infected with the virus only when they
stuck themselves with needles that had some of the
patients' blood on it, and even those cases are exceedingly rare.

There has been a lot of publicity about patients
picking up AIDS from infected doctors. As far as
anyone knows, there have been only five cases. All
seem to have occurred in Florida, originating from
one dentist who was apparently exceedingly careless,
and who himself died of AIDS. For a time there was
a controversy over whether physicians who perform
operations and other procedures that involve a lot of
blood should all be tested for HIV. The Centers for
Disease Control recently concluded that states will
decide on a case-by-case basis whether HIV-infected
physicians can continue practicing.

When AIDS was first identified, a number of

people had received transfusions with HIV-infected blood. A few hemophiliacs (individuals who have inherited a genetic disease that prevents their own blood from clotting) had become ill from something called the clotting factor, which helped to minimize their symptoms but was made of human blood products. Apparently the virus had made its way into the medication via infected blood. Today all blood used in transfusions and to make medicines is thoroughly tested, and the chances of getting AIDS from a transfusion is small. *Nobody can get AIDS from giving blood.*

As of November 1991, when Magic made his sad announcement, almost 200,000 people had already become seriously ill with AIDS-related diseases, and nearly 65 percent of those had died. AIDS is a plague that nobody should ignore. If you have done any of the things that are in the following list, you are at risk and should be tested no matter how young you are or how healthy you seem to be:

1. If you have had unprotected vaginal, anal, or oral sex (i.e., sex without a latex condom) with a partner whose sexual history you are not completely sure of. Remember that when you have sex with anyone, you also are having sex with every single person your partner has slept with within the past ten years, at least.

137

2. If you have had sex with multiple partners. That means either gay or straight sex, or both.
3. If you have used intravenous drugs and employed anything but a brand-new needle that had never been used by anyone else.
4. If you have had sex with a user of injected drugs or with someone who has previously had sex with a drug user.

Because AIDS is so terrifyingly dangerous, testing for HIV is available everywhere. In any city or town in the United States there are testing stations in hospitals, in clinics, and in public health departments. HIV-antibody tests are generally free and can be completely anonymous. Neither your parents nor anyone else will be notified that you have had the test or what the results were. As a matter of fact, you won't even be asked your name. You will be given a number, and you can find out your test results by telephoning or going to the test station and giving the doctor or counselor your number.

Should you test positive, you will definitely need counseling and medical care. Your test center will give you information on how to get this kind of help.

Here are some telephone numbers for further information about your possible risk of AIDS, where you can be tested, and what you need to know to get the test.

National Hot Lines

National AIDS Hotline (Centers for Disease Control)   1-800-342-AIDS

Provides information on AIDS and referrals for testing and counseling in your own community.

National STD Hotline (Centers for Disease Control)   1-800-227-8922

Provides information on sexually transmitted diseases, including HIV, and referrals for testing and treatment.

Local Telephone Numbers

Look in the white pages under Public Health Department of (your city or state) or (your city or state) Department of Public Health.

CHAPTER 14

AT HOME OR ON THE ROAD: OTHER SEXUALLY TRANSMITTED DISEASES

There was a time, not so very long ago, when most people thought that the spread of sexually transmitted diseases (STDs) was under control in the United States. The most frequently occurring, gonorrhea and syphilis, seemed to be easily cured by antibiotics, and the number of those newly infected was declining. Unfortunately, this trend has been reversed within the last few years, and the largest group acquiring these diseases are teenagers. Often they go untreated until they become seriously ill.

Girls, particularly, are at risk. Almost all sexually transmitted diseases are most serious for women who are not treated fairly promptly. These diseases can result in pelvic infections and in sterility. Experts estimate that a great many women who discover they cannot conceive were once infected with such a disease.

Most cases of gonorrhea and syphilis can still be cured with antibiotics, although a few strains have become more resistant than they were in the past. *All sexually transmitted diseases must be diagnosed and treated by a physician.* Too many teenagers who know that they respond to treatment with antibiotics tend to borrow a prescription from a friend to avoid having to go to a doctor or a clinic, have it filled, and take medication until the immediate symptoms have disappeared. That is about the most dangerous action one can take. In the first place, particularly in women, symptoms may not even appear at all, or may disappear on their own or with medication—only to return in much more serious form days, weeks, or months later. The diseases are then much more difficult to cure, and sterility may have already set in.

Boys usually know when they have gonorrhea. It's always uncomfortable and sometimes painful. Generally they either go to a doctor or try to get antibiotics on their own. But they may be symptom-free and still infectious unless they have completed a prescribed course of treatment, which almost never happens with self-medication. That means they can give the disease to their sexual partners, potentially ruining these young women's chances of ever having babies. Obviously, nobody has the right to do that, just to save themselves the time and possible embarrassment of seeing a doctor.

Syphilis is even more serious than gonorrhea and, unfortunately, is more difficult to self-diagnose. It can be treated in the early stages with antibiotics and cured promptly. It seemed on its way out, so many states no longer require premarital blood tests to make sure that couples won't give the disease to each other or their unborn children. But within the past five years, public health authorities have been appalled at the speed with which this STD has made its way back. Those mainly affected are teenagers and people in their early twenties. Many states are now considering reviving laws to mandate premarital STD testing, since at least 500,000 people in the United States are now estimated to be infected and getting no treatment.

One of the problems with syphilis is what some doctors call its "sneaky nature." Syphilis comes in three stages. Usually it starts with a small ulcer or pimplelike eruption on the site of the infection. In some women this symptom may occur internally. It's usually not painful and goes away on its own; therefore, it may never be noticed. However, this is the most curable form of the infection.

During the second stage, the infected person may have a sore throat and a rash, symptoms that mimic the flu. At that point the bacteria that cause syphilis, known as spirochetes, have invaded the bloodstream. The disease still curable at this stage but may require a more lengthy course of treatment. But, again, the symptoms will go away with no treatment at all. By the time the patient reaches the third stage, he or she may no longer be contagious, except to an unborn child, but the spirochetes have taken up permanent lodging in several organs in the body, including the liver, the heart, and the brain. Once these organs have been damaged, there is no way to repair them. Patients then die of heart attacks, liver disease, or brain disorders. Not so long ago back wards of mental hospitals were filled with middle-aged or elderly men and women who had gone mad from untreated syphilis, and who usually died in the hospitals. Unless we become aware that the disease is back among us in ever-increasing numbers, those wards may fill up again twenty or thirty years from now.

There are other STDs that are not as deadly as syphilis, but they too can damage our bodies or make our lives uncomfortable for many years. Genital herpes is another of these diseases that has reached epidemic proportions in the United States. Indeed, before AIDS became the principal concern, herpes got quite a lot of press, including cover stories in *Newsweek* and *Time*. The fact that we hear so little about genital herpes these days does not mean that it is no longer present, or even that its spread has abated. It's simply not nearly as worrisome as other diseases, although it too is to date incurable. Nobody

143

has ever died of genital herpes, however. It is only very painful and embarrassing, and during its acute stages (which recur periodically), highly contagious.

During the acute stage, the patient will suffer from painful sores in the genital area, plus flulike symptoms and sometimes a high fever. None of these symptoms respond to antibiotics, which work on bacteria; herpes is a virus. However, treatment with antiviral drugs, which also have to be prescribed by a physician, can make the sores less painful and possibly limit the number of outbreaks. The disease is infectious while there is any indication of soreness. It can also present a danger to babies during the birth process and may require the mother to undergo a cesarean section in order to deliver a healthy child.

Two other STDs, chlamydia and pelvic inflammatory disease, are generally symptomless in males but easily detected in women. The former STD shows up as a profuse vaginal discharge in women, with itching and burning, and the latter with acute, severe pain in the pelvic area and fever. Both require expert diagnosis since they are often confused with other diseases, and both can result in permanent female sterility. The male partner of a woman with either of these conditions must also be treated, even though he does not show symptoms, since he still carries the infection and will reinfect his sexual partner even after she has been cured (or, for that matter, infect new partners) unless he, too, has been completely cured.

With a suspicion of STDs, when in doubt, get medical help. Even something that seems minor during the first days or weeks may turn into a major illness without treatment.

Here are the best sources of help:

National Hot Lines

National STD Hotline   1-800-227-8922
Provides information on sexually transmitted diseases and referrals for testing and treatment in your own community.

Local Telephone Numbers

Look in the white pages under Department of Health of (your city or county) or (your city or county) Department of Health.

Remember, all questions, diagnoses, and treatment programs are completely confidential. You will be asked to notify all recent sexual partners, since they, too, must be tested and, if necessary, treated, but one would expect that anyone who feels that he may have given a serious disease to someone else would want to do this anyhow.

MEDICAL EMERGENCIES:
WHEN TO GET HELP FAST

Anyone away from home—adults, adolescents, and especially teenagers—might have a difficult time getting needed medical help, no matter how serious their condition may seem. Anyone without medical insurance will almost certainly be turned away from the offices of private physicians, many hospitals, and even some emergency rooms. However, there are ways to get help, especially if the problem looks as if it may be a serious infectious disease. The vast majority of cities and/or states are even more afraid of an epidemic of contagious disease than they are of bankruptcy.

Here are some of the symptoms for which help should be sought immediately. If one source of such help (an emergency room, for instance) refuses to respond because you have no money or health insurance, look for another one.

1. *A severe hacking cough* that has persisted for more than two weeks. There is the possibility of tuberculosis, which is reappearing in epidemic proportions throughout the United States, especially among street people in homeless shelters and in prisons. Good sources for free TB tests are local health departments, free clinics, the emergency rooms of city or county

hospitals, or health stations in shelters for the homeless, if these shelters provide such services in your community.

2. *Night sweats, sudden and extreme weight loss, a high fever, persistent diarrhea, mouth sores that seem to persist for longer than two weeks, genital sores.* One or more of these conditions may be caused by a sexually transmitted disease, including AIDS. Tests are generally available, free of charge, and completely confidential, at local health departments, free clinics, and some city or county hospitals. Hot lines for additional information are listed at the ends of Chapters 13 and 14, dealing with AIDS and other sexually transmitted diseases.

3. *A sore throat* that seems to get worse after a few days and may be accompanied by a high fever. This symptom may signal a staphylococcus infection, which can result in rheumatic fever, a damaged heart, and other serious problems, besides being easily spread through casual contact. Sources of help are free clinics and/ or emergency rooms of city or county hospitals.

4. *Animal bites*, including bites by rats, dogs, cats, and other mammals. Insect bites are generally not considered emergencies; they are just annoying and uncomfortable. However, bites by a mammal might produce rabies, for which immediate treatment is required. Untreated rabies

147

can be deadly. Sources of help are hospital emergency rooms and free clinics.

5. *Any accident that involves an injury to the head.* A fall, a blow, or any other occurrence that results in temporary loss of consciousness, persistent dizziness, or double vision should be investigated promptly. Even if the symptoms don't produce a coma or some other very alarming result, there may be internal bleeding or a severe concussion that might result in permanent brain damage or death. The best source of help is the nearest emergency room.

CHAPTER 15

GETTING OFF THE STREET

There comes a time when almost all teenagers who have spent time in the streets feel that they have had enough. Often they just don't know where to turn to get help in getting back to their homes or, if that seems impossible, into some safe, permanent shelter.

Dealing with the problem is easiest for those teenagers who have decided that home is the best place for them. There are any number of agencies that will get in touch with parents or other relatives, and arrange for transportation. If some kind of counseling or mediation is needed, most of these agencies have experts to work with the runaway and the family to make the transition back to home ground as easy for everybody as possible.

For this kind of situation, the Covenant House Nineline may be the best choice. The number, which is also listed elsewhere in this book, is 1-800-999-9999. Calls are free. You don't even have to put any money in the pay phone. Just dial the number or ask an operator to call it for you. Covenant House also has offices in five U. S. and one Canadian city, where a counselor will be able to discuss each individual situation and make suggestions on how to proceed. Offices are located in New York, New York; Houston, Texas; Fort Lauderdale, Florida; New Orleans, Louisiana; Anchorage, Alaska; and Toronto, Canada.

The counselor will also help a runaway who does not have money for a ticket home, health problems that should be dealt with before a trip is contemplated, or any other difficulties.

Financial assistance is generally available if neither the teenager nor the family can afford to buy a ticket home. A health exam can also often be arranged. If the teenager has had a minor problem with the police, legal help may also be given. If there is a major legal problem, there may have to be a court hearing before a runaway is allowed to leave the state.

Other agencies that can be helpful are the local YMCA and YWCA, a family service agency affiliated with Family Service America, or Travelers Aid, which has offices at many airports, railroad stations, and bus terminals.

Runaways between the ages of twelve and seventeen may also be able to receive transportation home free of charge through the Greyhound-Trailways bus program, which is sponsored jointly by this company and the International Association of Chiefs of Police. However, using this program means going to a local police station. The police will confirm the information the runaway gives them. The parents will be notified and must agree that they are willing to take the teenager back. The police will then let the family know of their runaway's arrival time, will accompany the homebound youngster to the bus terminal just before departure time, and will fill out a form for a nonrefundable ticket. Usually the accompanying police officer will also let the bus driver know that this passenger should not be allowed to leave the bus before his or her destination has been reached.

This may seem like an easy way to get a ticket home, but it means registering with the police, and as mentioned previously, running away from home is considered an act of juvenile delinquency in some jurisdictions. A record of the whole transaction may be kept. So, if at all possible, an agency such as Covenant House, which keeps all matters related to the family situation confidential, may be a better choice.

Teenagers who want to get off the streets, but who for reasons they know best don't want to return to their families, should probably turn to private agencies, rather than police departments or other public authorities. Certainly teenagers who have been sexually or physically abused, and do not want to report the situation, may feel that a return home will be as bad or worse than continuing to live in the streets. Shelters, foster care, group homes, and other resources are possibilities for them. So again, a private, nonprofit agency is the best resource. There is Covenant House, and in some cities there are other similar organizations. For instance, in Los Angeles, beside Covenant House, there is Children of the Night (look in the Los Angeles phone book), and in Boston, at the time this book was written, there was an excellent agency called Bridge Over Troubled Waters.

All of these organizations are especially set up for kids who know that they cannot, or have decided they will not, return home. Calling and making an appointment for a counseling session does not mean that anyone will be forced to take an action against his or her will. The conversation with the counselor is confidential, and families will not be notified unless the teenager agrees. Nor will the police be informed. All of these agencies know the resources in their own communities and will try to help anyone who does not know what to do next or where to go to find the best possible solution to his or her problems.

From what many of the teenage runaways say and the kinds of stories they have to tell, many who have been on their own for months or years have good reasons for having left abusive or otherwise harmful home situations. However, some left because of misunderstandings that might have been worked out, and have not returned because they are too proud to admit that they may have made a mistake. Pride is a very poor reason to live in continuous misery and danger. Anyone who stays in the streets mainly because he or she is too proud to ask parents or other relatives for permission to come home should definitely discuss the situation with a counselor, and get help in mending fences. A call to the Covenant House Nineline is a good first step.

CHAPTER 16

WHAT'S HAPPENED TO THEM ALL?

In November of 1991, just before this book was finished, I made an attempt to find some of the teenagers whom I had come to know during the previous two years who seemed to have disappeared from the places where they had made their temporary and usually illegal homes. Most of them appeared to have vanished. No agency, no police officers, not even some of the street children who now lived near the places where I had found, talked to, shared meals with, and—as often as they would let me—tried to help the runaways, seemed to know where most of them had gone.

Little Beau, the twelve-year-old who picked up older men on Second Avenue in New York near the United Nations, and who paid for my hamburger because, he assured me, he made more money than I did, seemed to have vanished without a trace. Since I had liked him, worried about him, and hoped that somehow he would find a better life (even with less money), I spent more time looking for him than for anybody else. The police officers who were now patrolling what had been his area could not even remember him. I called agencies, hospitals, and talked to other boys and girls like him who were hanging out nearby to learn if anyone had seen him. Nobody had.

What could have happened to a young boy like Beau? Unfortunately, the chances are that, if he was still alive, he was either very sick or in a juvenile detention center. He had no home to which he could have gone. He was too proud and too independent to accept help.

Sometimes, walking on Second Avenue late at night, I thought I saw him and called his name. But it was always someone else . . . another young boy trying to make his way in New York, who in two years would probably also have disappeared.

None of the teenagers who lived and worked in the Times Square area were there any longer either. Times Square is undergoing redevelopment. Buildings in which groups of homeless kids once lived have been torn down. When the city will have enough money to build some of the planned apartment houses, theaters, and offices in those empty and boarded-up spaces is not known. If most cities in the

United States are short of cash, New York is broke.

The house where the New York group once made its temporary home was a pile of rubble. One police officer who has walked the beat on Eighth Avenue between Forty-second and Fifty-second streets for years remembered the kids who lived there, bought take-out fried chicken for a Thanksgiving dinner, found an abandoned, scraggly tree on Christmas and decorated it, and tried to go trick-or-treating on Halloween because they considered themselves a family. He said that when the old apartment house in which they lived fell to the wrecker, the kids tried to rescue some of their few belongings, but they started too late. Their mattresses, lamps, oil stove, and even the television set that the youngest member of the group, Junior, had found, had been buried by bricks and cement. The officer thought that some of the members of the group might have come in out of the cold, i.e., gone to Covenant House, which is on the same street, or some other agency that helps homeless kids. He may just have been trying to cheer me up, because another officer said, "Nothing good ever happens to any of these kids."

That's not quite true, because both Aggie and Lucinda apparently landed on their feet.

Aggie was still working days at the same restaurant where I found her, and she had achieved her ambition. She was going to an excellent school for chefs at night on money she had been able to borrow from her employers and on a scholarship awarded by the school. She had a larger apartment in a somewhat better neighborhood and had even managed to get her younger roommate to register for the local public school, where she was getting a high school diploma at night while helping out in Aggie's workplace during the day. Both girls looked healthy, clean, and happy.

One evening, when I was watching a modern dance company performing at City Center, a theater that specializes in dance, I was sure I saw Lucinda. I went backstage to talk to her. She also had finished high school at the School of Performing Arts near Lincoln Center, where she had danced as a street performer. After school she had auditioned for several shows and had finally managed to get a job as an understudy for a chorus girl in a musical. Unfortunately, the musical closed after a few weeks. She then auditioned for several dance companies and was accepted as an apprentice in an excellent one. I saw her in a very small part, dancing with the same energy and obvious talent that she had shown on the street corner. She hoped to become a full-fledged company member within the year. "I made more money dancing on the street," she said. "Dancers in this kind of company are not paid a lot. But dancing is what I want, and the teaching here is excellent. I rent a room with one of the other apprentices. I get enough to eat. I take class every day, and I have health insurance. What more could anyone ask? Well, perhaps a raise in pay."

When I was last in California, I did meet Elvis and King on the beach in Venice. It was fall, and too cold and damp to live under the boardwalk. The first thing they told me was that they had changed their names. "Every other boy around here is called either Elvis or King," they said. "We needed a more special identity." They called themselves Rock and Rex. Otherwise, little had changed for them. Like the members of the New York group, they were trying to find an abandoned house in which to hunker down for the winter. They still coughed, were much too thin, and looked as if they were in serious need of medical attention. Neither was prepared to go to a clinic. When they had enough money, they bought cough medicine. More often they used the few dollars they got panhandling or running errands for a variety of dubious characters to buy drugs. Both insisted that they only snorted heroin and cocaine, but there were needle tracks on their arms. It was obvious that they were not going to be able to make it on the street much longer. Indeed, they might not be able to make it at all.

They did, however, have news of Vlad, Maria, and Debbie. It seems that as the birth of Maria's baby neared, Vlad decided to call his parents one more time. He finally told them that he was married to Maria, and that she was expecting their child momentarily. His parents, although still completely opposed to his girl and his life-style, urged him to come home, and finally allowed him to bring Maria. Elvis, now called "Rock," said that they had called Vlad's parents' house once. Maria had had a baby girl who was surprisingly healthy, and, although her family refused to accept her, her husband's parents had become reconciled to the situation. The two were temporarily living with them, and Vlad was looking for a job. He was eighteen and no longer a minor. He had also obtained a high school equivalency certificate and hoped that soon he would find some kind of employment that would allow him, Maria, and the baby to find an inexpensive room or small apartment somewhere, so that they could live on their own as a family.

Debbie had also had her baby, in a public hospital in Los Angeles. Since she was a minor and had no place to go, the welfare department had placed the baby in a foster home and found a shelter for Debbie. She hated it there. Occasionally, she came back to Venice and joined Elvis and King on the beach. She also wanted her baby back, but, of course, there was not a chance that she'd get her little boy unless she could prove that she had a suitable home for him. That seemed an unlikely possibility, since Debbie was still a minor, had no job nor any prospect of getting one, and therefore no money for rent, food, health

159

care, or even an occasional diaper. She talked about just picking up the baby and running away. Elvis and King had told her that this was a crazy idea. She could lose the child permanently and land in a juvenile detention center or in jail herself. "We tell her that taking the child away from the foster home could be considered kidnapping, but she doesn't understand how anyone could charge her with kidnapping her own child," King said. "Debbie is a very loving girl, but she is not very smart."

The boys thought that Blossom was picked up by a police officer and might be in a psychiatric ward or hospital. "She went completely off the wall when Vlad and Maria left town," Elvis said. "You know, she had actually talked herself into believing that they were her parents." One could only hope that Blossom, somehow, would get the help she needed for her serious emotional problems, and that she would find the home for which she had been searching so desperately almost all her young life.

That leaves Don and me. Don, the boy who lived with us when a juvenile judge told him that he would have to find a respectable home or be sent to a detention center, finished college. He took some additional courses in art, specializing in antiques. He now works for one of New York's large auction houses as an expert appraiser, and when I spoke to him hoped to be sent to Paris for a year to find French antiques. "They are all the rage now," he said. "Perhaps if I find some interesting piece of porcelain, I'll bring it back to you." He may just do it. After all, he split all that wood for me after my husband died, and nobody has ever tried to rob my Connecticut house after he burglarproofed it.

As for me . . . I just finished writing this book.